Nichola Boughe~ ~~~~~~ ~y
Colette Roberts • Sarah Webb

Series editors: Martin Collier • Rosemary Rees

Planning and Resource Pack 2

www.heinemann.co.uk

✓ Free online support
✓ Useful weblinks
✓ 24 hour online ordering

01865 888080

Heinemann is an imprint of Pearson Education Limited, a company incorporated in England and Wales, having its registered office at Edinburgh Gate, Harlow, Essex, CM20 2JE. Registered company number: 872828

www.heinemann.co.uk

Heinemann is the registered trademark of Pearson Education Limited.

Text © Pearson Education Limited 2008

First published 2008

12 11 10 09 08
10 9 8 7 6 5 4 3 2 1

British Library Cataloguing in Publication Data is available from the British Library on request.

ISBN 978 0 435318 95 6

Typesetting by TechType
Illustrations by Tek Art
Original illustrations © Pearson Education Ltd 2008
Cover photo © Birmingham Museums and Art Gallery
Printed in the UK by Ashford Colour Press Ltd

Websites
There are links to relevant websites in this book. In order to ensure that the links are up-to-date, that the links work, and that the sites are not inadvertently linked to sites that could be considered offensive, we have made the links available on the Heinemann website at www.heinemann.co.uk/hotlinks. When you access the site, the express code is 8956T.

Contents

Introduction

Rationale behind the course

History in Progress has been written to help teachers deliver the requirements of the revised History National Curriculum Key Stage 3 Programme of Study. The course incorporates all of the new strands included in the revised Programme of Study including an emphasis on enquiry and diversity. *History in Progress* is a course devised for pupils studying in the twenty-first century.

History in Progress has been planned and written with the following wider curriculum and school issues in mind.

- The individual child comes first. *History in Progress* takes into account the priorities from the *Every Child Matters* agenda by providing for the individuals' needs, through a range of well-structured tasks and focused success criteria in every lesson.
- The course caters for a very broad range of pupils' abilities. There is clear differentiation through both task and outcome providing an appropriate challenge to learners of all abilities. The books and assessment tasks are structured in such a way so as to provide stretch and challenge for all learners, not just the most able.
- *History in Progress* has been structured to facilitate the aims of the Secondary National Strategy to deliver teaching and learning of the highest quality. Each enquiry is focused on specific learning objectives, with clear outcomes based on the principles of 'All … Most … Some …'.
- The course is flexible, providing a variety of pathways through the Key Stage 3 History curriculum.
- It is understood that there is time constraint on the amount of time given to History at Key Stage 3 so *History in Progress* provides opportunities for the delivery of History through cross-curricular initiatives as well as a distinct discipline.
- It has been devised with the classroom of the twenty-first century in mind and takes full account of changing technologies, both in terms of delivery of the course and pupils' work. There are ICT links built in throughout the course to help pupils process data research information and successfully present their findings.
- Citizenship is an important element of the curriculum. *History in Progress* provides opportunities to deliver Citizenship through a historical context, both in terms of content and pupils' skills.
- *History in Progress* promotes a variety of learning approaches. There is an emphasis on individualised learning, problem solving and discovery. There are also opportunities in every enquiry for visual and kinaesthetic learning. Additionally, pupils encouraged to work in pairs and groups, and a range of strategies are suggested throughout this Planning and Resource Pack to allow for this.
- The course has been devised to promote tolerance and diversity both through its content and the learning processes.
- The Pupil Book is complemented by detailed lesson plans in the Planning and Resource Pack, which have been designed so that the lessons can be delivered by either a subject specialist or a non-subject specialist.
- *History in Progress* aims to enhance the pupils' literacy and communication skills through activities that encourage a range of outcomes – speaking, role play, extended writing, presentations, debate.

History in Progress was planned and written to address the following History-specific issues.

- The course provides overview alongside opportunity for the study of history in themes and in depth.
- It has been devised with the aim of promoting pupil interest in and enthusiasm for History.
- The content of the course and the ways in which that content is tackled aims to make History relevant to all pupils.
- It is hoped that following the *History in Progress* scheme will provide the impetus

for pupils to opt to continue to study History at Key Stage 4.

- Through introducing meaningful cross-cultural links and the cross-curricular initiatives outlined earlier, *History in Progress* attempts to instil a greater understanding of context and a greater sense of period.
- Throughout the course, there is a greater emphasis on source work as part of a wider historical enquiry as recommended by the Historical Association 14–19 Curriculum Report.
- The course promotes chronological understanding and encourages pupils to build a chronological framework of periods studied in which new knowledge can be contextualised.
- Pupils are encouraged to identify and explain change and continuity within and across periods of history and are presented with ample opportunities to analyse and explain the reasons for and results of historical events, situations and changes.
- *History in Progress* aims to provide clarity around historical interpretations and significance in history, providing enquiries that allow pupils to focus on these concepts.
- Pupils are encouraged to make links and connections between topics of study both within and across time periods, countries and themes.

Key features of *History in Progress*

History

The aim of *History in Progress* is to make History both attractive and relevant to pupils. The enquiries have been selected and written with the aim of stimulating the pupils' imagination, thereby drawing them in to the subject. History is and must remain relevant to young people. *History in Progress* aims to bring History alive so that pupils can identify with the subject.

The history in the series looks at the past from a range of perspectives. It balances the study of national and international affairs with a focus on the personal and the local. The series shows through comparison and a broad perspective that all history needs to be understood in a wider context; that the history of a locality cannot be fully grasped without an understanding of the larger national and international context.

The series also aims to draw the pupils into the process of history. The enquiries have been designed in such a way that the pupils will understand that history is a discipline based on enquiry, interpretation and decision-making. It is hoped that pupils will understand that the process of history relies on discussion and debate.

History in Progress has been written to help prepare pupils for life after school. From the start of the series, it emphasises the diversity and fluidity of society hundreds of years ago. The series promotes citizenship, both in terms of the history studied but also the processes of debate, negotiation and voting that are integral to a number of the activities. The series stresses the historical diversity of the national community and the links and interdependence within the international community.

Structure

The curriculum has been structured through the combination of the key concepts, key processes and identified areas of study. The Programme of Study suggests a number of areas of study. These have been rationalised into three defining themes of study:

- Ruling
- Living and working
- Moving and travelling.

Through studying all units, the pupils are working through the key concepts identified in the revised Programme of Study – see pages 12–17. They gain extensive experience of working with evidence as part of an historical enquiry and communicating their ideas in a clear and structured fashion.

Unit 1: Ruling

This unit focuses on the shift in power from the early sixteenth century to the start of the twentieth century. The unit is broken up into enquiries that are set out in a chronological framework. The enquiries focus predominantly on the major periods, events and strands in English and then British history, but there is also the opportunity to reflect on the changes in England and Britain in the wider context of European and world history, for example by exploring the revolutions in America and France and comparing the outcomes of these to the changes brought about by the Civil War in England. Pupils also have the chance to investigate the closer relationship and eventual union between England and Scotland.

Unit 2: Living and working

This unit explores in detail the changes that took place in people's everyday lives during this period. There is a focus on technological change, the growth of towns and cities and the impact this had on health and law and order.

The unit picks up themes from *History in Progress 1* such as leisure time and care for the poor. Pupils also have the chance to explore life in other cultures with enquiries focusing on China and American Indians.

Unit 3: Moving and travelling

This unit is underpinned by the growth of the British Empire and there are enquiries focusing on this at the start and end of the unit. Within that overarching framework, pupils have the chance to explore one of the other key requirements of the Programme of Study, the slave trade. Links can be made back to *History in Progress 1* which looked at the slave trade in Tudor times. The movement of people and goods changed enormously in this period, and pupils have the chance to find out about the impact that steam had on transport; about explorers such as Cook and Franklin; and reasons why people were forced to emigrate in lessons on the Highland Clearances and the Irish Potato Famine.

Carefully levelled tasks

Each enquiry includes a progression of colour-coded tasks. The colouring of each task is so that teachers and pupils can identify the national curriculum level. This system has been designed to facilitate ongoing assessment and effective tracking of the pupils' progress.

Different levels of tasks are offered to promote pupil choice and encourage them to select their own individual learning pathways. The system can also be used to challenge all pupils to work at a higher level.

This is the key to the colour coding throughout the *History in Progress* series.

	Year 7	Year 8	Year 9
Green tasks	level 4	level 4/5	level 5
Blue tasks	level 4/5	level 5	level 5/6
Orange tasks	level 5	level 5/6	level 6
Purple tasks	level 5/6	level 6	level 7

Taking it further!

'Taking it further!' features within the Pupil Books provide pupils with further stretch and challenge and can be used in a number of ways:

- as extension work in class
- as distinct lessons for more able classes
- as homework exercises to build on skills, knowledge and concepts learned in class.

Some 'Taking it further!' sections attempt to deal with controversies and provoke discussion and debate. Others enquires have been left open to encourage further research work and independent learning.

Back to the start

At the end of the many of the enquiries, 'Back to the start' can be used to serve a number of purposes.

- It can be used as part of the plenary to direct pupils' attention back to the main themes.

- In some cases it directs pupils to reflect on overarching concepts that cover more than one enquiry.

'Back to the start' can be used to encourage pupils to reflect not only on the content covered but also on the processes undertaken and the skills practised through the course of the enquiry.

Making connections

'Making connections', at the end of each unit, draw together some of the dominant themes in that unit. They can be used as whole lessons, and lesson plans are provided in the Planning and Resource Pack.

Alternatively, the 'Making connections' exercises can be used as the starting point for a research project that allows pupils to explore the identified themes and concepts in greater detail.

Skillsbank

A 'Skillsbank' has been provided at the end of the Pupil Book; it can be used in several different ways:

- to provide support for pupils needing additional practice in specific skills
- to enable pupils to extend their range of skills-based understandings and competencies
- to add to the range of accessible homework tasks
- to provide a point of reference for pupils working individually or in groups
- to enable development of those skills targeted by GCSE History examinations.

Assessment

Accurate and effective assessment is a central component of *History in Progress*. Indeed, an opportunity for assessment of the pupils' progress is integrated into every enquiry. The course encourages a balance of formal assessment, through the inclusion of assessment tasks at the end of each unit, and ongoing informal assessment.

Such informal assessment is an essential component in the tracking of pupil progress and recognition of an individual's improved performance. It will help in identifying each pupil's

strengths and weaknesses and will inform strategies for further progress. It will also help teachers to set individual targets for pupils.

Teachers are not expected to provide a level for every piece of work. However, the innovative assessment structure provided by *History in Progress* through the colour-coded, levelled tasks enables the teacher to quickly and accurately judge levels of current performance.

The formal and informal assessment tasks completed throughout each unit will provide teachers with the evidence to support an overall judgement as to the level of each pupil's performance.

The assessment tasks in each unit explain the tasks clearly, provide instructions on what pupils should do, and offer hints, tips and suggestions to get them started. Further support is provided in the accompanying teacher notes in the Planning and Resource Pack. The markschemes in the Planning and Resource Pack provide a pupil-friendly approach to assessing their work, and encourage target setting and reflection.

Peer- and self-assessment

There are opportunities throughout the course for peer and self assessment. Plenaries in particular have been designed to encourage self-review not only of knowledge but also of how pupils have learned and participated in the lesson. Below is a list suggestions for including pupils in the assessment process.

- Provide opportunities for pupils to respond to teacher and peer marking.
- Give them a chance to assess their own work before the teacher.
- Provide opportunities for analysis of existing markschemes.
- Encourage pupils to devise their own markschemes for activities.

Learning strategies

Thinking skills throughout *History in Progress*

A wide variety of different approaches to the development of thinking skills is provided throughout *History in Progress*. Pupils are invited to explore, examine and investigate, to empathise, appreciate, debate and reflect. The ways in which these essential thinking skills can be developed further are suggested in the Planning and Resource Pack. Although, here, these skills are history orientated, they are transferable to other subjects and disciplines.

Think pair share

Many of the tasks in *History in Progress 1* can be carried out in this way. This approach ensures that all pupils have had chance to consider their response to a question. They will have already thought about it and tried it out on their partner and should be able to answer if asked by the teacher. This strategy can also eliminate the need for hands up, as asking for answers from a range of pupils is likely to result in a range of considered responses.

Snowballing

This is a way to encourage sharing of ideas and development of response among pupils. Pose a question or suggest a discussion point and ask pupils to work individually to record their response. They then work with a partner to develop a shared response, then in a group of four to develop a common answer, and so on as appropriate. At each stage they should incorporate the best ideas from the previous responses, thus encouraging ongoing reflection and refinement of the ideas. Take whole-class feedback when the group work has been completed.

Gimme 5

The aim of this is for pupils to recall information and recap learning. As pupils come in the classroom ask them to write five ideas connected to a particular topic. These can then be shared in pairs, groups or with the whole class.

Quick-fire questions

A useful starter activity, this can be used to recap learning from a previous lesson before moving on to develop that knowledge and understanding. Prepare a list of questions, preferably with short answers, on a topic and go round the class asking for responses. Pupils should aim to keep their answers as short and to the point as possible and to respond quickly to the question. Alternatively, you could ask pupils to prepare questions that

can then be asked by either the teacher or by the pupil.

Vote with your feet

Pupils position themselves by moving to stand along a continuum, across the classroom or along one wall, to show their opinion about a subject or their strength of feeling for or against a particular question or issue. This can be done once, when new information is introduced, and then done again to see whether pupils have, literally, shifted their position.

Mysteries

Mysteries (e.g. **Lesson 2.1c** Great Fire of London: accident or arson?) that focus around a key question can be used to develop problem-solving skills. Pupils have to evaluate a range of evidence and possible responses and suggest a solution to the problem. They are an effective way of involving pupils in higher order thinking skills such as classification, speculation and testing hypotheses. In a reversal of roles, you might want to ask pupils to devise their own mysteries, coming up with a key question connected to a topic they have been studying and then suggesting evidence for analysis either from *History in Progress* or other sources.

Differentiation

Differentiation is provided in a variety of different ways to be used as appropriate.

- **Differentiation by task** is encouraged by the use of colour-coded tasks linked to specific levels. Lower achievers are supported by the provision, in the Planning and Resource Pack, of writing frames and thinking grids. The 'Taking it further!' sections provide stretch and challenge for the more able pupils. Again, the use of these is further supported by the Planning and Resource Pack.

- **Differentiation by outcome** is enabled by the provision of 'levelled' markschemes. These have been written in a pupil-friendly way so that peer review and individual challenge are both possible ways of assessing pupil achievement. The Planning and Resource Pack provides appropriate grids for pupils to complete that enable them to reflect on their achievement and progress and to consider what they have to do to move up within a level or move up a complete level.

Cross-curricular links

Many of the enquiries can provide cross-curricular links and these can be developed by the teacher if appropriate within the curriculum of individual schools.

Subject	Examples of linking lessons
PSHE	1.2b, 1.8
Citizenship	1.4, 2.8, 3.7
RE	2.5, 3.4, 3.6
English	3.4
Geography	3.9

Inclusion

The *History in Progress* course is designed to provide effective learning opportunities for all pupils. The layout of each unit, the use of pictures and colour-coding and the staged assessment tasks are all designed to make the series accessible to all pupils. The choice of content in the course has been made in such a way as to enhance the recognition of cultural diversity as something of value for all learners. The range of tasks and variety of design and layout are offered in such a way as to cater for pupils with different learning styles. The approaches to teaching and learning will motivate pupils of both genders from different social backgrounds.

History in Progress is supported by a Planning and Resource Pack that includes worksheets that can be used to support learners with specific learning difficulties. The 'Taking it further!' features aim to stretch and engage the more able learners but can be used to provide all pupils with alternative activities as appropriate.

The use of ICT and the ICT support materials further ensure that the course is open to all learners.

Using ICT

There are opportunities throughout *History in Progress* for pupils to use ICT to support and extend their learning. It can be used as an information source, to search for and select relevant information and evidence, and to present and refine their work. Many of the activities lend themselves to ICT ranging from the use of Word or PowerPoint to present written work to the use of Microsoft Publisher to create posters and displays.

Suggestions for further research using the Internet have been made throughout the Planning and Resource Pack in the lesson plans. However, it is important that pupils develop skills that enable them to review information from the internet critically.

The LiveText CD-ROM that accompanies each Pupil Book contains a wide variety of additional activities and models that will enhance pupils' thinking and learning in History.

Local history

An important element of the new National Curriculum History is a focus on local history. It is important that pupils have an opportunity to investigate local history as part of their Key Stage 3 studies. Engagement with local sources and visits to local sites of significance are fundamental in helping the pupils appreciate the relevance of the past to their own lives.

History in Progress has been designed in such a way to stimulate the delivery of local history. The course is structured in a way that gives teachers and pupils the opportunity to explore the history of their localities.

There are plenty of opportunities in *History in Progress* for pupils to engage in local history. These are some examples:

The emphasis placed on urban life in the nineteenth century could lead to a research project centred on how their local environment changed in the nineteenth century. The pupils could research changes in the physical environment including the building of houses as well as public buildings.

Some places may well have a standing workhouse or almshouses from the nineteenth century. Pupils might be encouraged to find out about the history of poor relief in their locality by using local records. The National Trust has restored the workhouse at Southwell in Nottinghamshire and it provides an excellent day out for schools within reach. If a visit to Southwell is not possible, pupils can access information about the workhouse via www.heinemann.co.uk/hotlinks.

Those schools that are situated towards the coast may profitably explore local links with exploration and the slave trade. Many parish churches include memorials to people who were involved in imperial exploits. Likewise, many museums will have records of local people who helped build the British Empire.

The unit on the impact of the railway opens up the possibility of project work based on a local railway station. Many towns and villages no longer have stations but there is still physical evidence of the railways with bridges, cuttings and embankments visible. Those schools near York might be able to provide the pupils with an opportunity to visit the fantastic National Railway Museum. For those schools unable to travel to York, pupils might be encouraged to visit the National Railway Museum's website. This can be accessed through www.heinemann.co.uk/hotlinks.

The above suggestions are just examples. There is considerable scope for other local history enquiries. Pupils might be encouraged to investigate the history of migration into their locality. This might include inviting representatives of immigrant communities into their schools to tell pupils the history of their community and answer questions.

Setting up an enquiry

As part of their work at Key Stage 3, pupils should be encouraged set up and follow their own structured enquiries. *History in Progress* provides a range of opportunities for pupils to do this.

- Before setting up an enquiry, make sure that pupils understand the terms and conditions of the enquiry with regards to structure, subject content and possible outcomes.
- Ensure that pupils are clear about how to devise questions that will form the basis of an hypothesis. One way of devising these questions is to use a statement followed by question stems such as 'To what extent do you agree with this statement?' or 'How far do you agree with this statement?' (See text that follows.)
- Advise pupils on where they might find relevant and appropriate information for their research. They should be encouraged to use reference books, the Internet, visit the school or local library.
- As in any enquiry, encourage pupils to consider both sides of a hypothesis before coming to their conclusion. As part of the conclusion, pupils should outline the evidence that supports either side before coming to a conclusion.
- The outcome to an enquiry can be presented in a number of ways from through written work, wall displays or as oral presentations.

What question shall I ask?

Once pupils have read through the information they should then attempt to set up an enquiry. This is best done through the asking of questions

Exemplar enquiry

Here is an example of a set enquiry that has come out of one of the units in *History in Progress* Book 2. Pupils have been set the following task, based on a study of the information in Enquiries 2.5, 2.7 and 3.6: 'To find out about the impact of industrialisation on Britain'

After considering the above issue, the pupils have then suggested the following hypothesis:

'By 1900 the way that people lived and worked in Britain had been greatly changed by steam power'.

To what extent do you agree with this statement?

Overview of *History in Progress – Book 2 (Year 8)*

The following grid outlines how *History in Progress – Book 2* has been designed to provide full support for the Programme of Study.

Enquiry	Chronological focus	Lessons	Key concepts and processes	Content	Cross-curriculum dimensions
Unit 1 Ruling					
1.1 What was the English Civil War?	1603–1649	a) The world turned upside down	1.2 Diversity; 1.4 Cause/consequence	3d, g	Identity and cultural diversity
		b) Charles I and the road to war	1.4 Cause/consequence	3d	
		c) King or parliament?	1.6c Interpretations; 2.2a, b Evidence	3d	
		d) Eyewitness: Naseby	1.4 Cause/consequence; 2.2a, b Evidence	3d	
		e) Taking it further!: How to punish a king	1.6c Interpretations; 2.1a, b Enquiry	3d	
1.2 Who should be in charge?	1649–1688	a) Parliament or king?	1.3 Change/continuity	3d, g	Identity and cultural diversity
		b) England invaded!	1.6c Interpretations; 2.1a, b Enquiry; 2.2a, b Evidence	3d	
1.3 Scotland and England: a popular union?	1707–1745	a) Were the Scottish MPs bribed?	1.6c Interpretations; 2.2a,b Evidence	3e	Identity and cultural diversity
		b) Was Bonnie Prince Charlie brave or foolish?	1.6c Interpretations; 2.2a Evidence	3e	
1.4 The Chinese Qing: a forgotten empire?		a) China: the 'Middle Kingdom'	2.2a, b Evidence	3h, i	Global dimension
		b) How was China ruled?	1.5 Significance	3i	
1.5 Who wanted their liberty and why?	1781–1793	a) Yorktown and the end of British North America	1.4 Cause/consequence	3i	Global dimension Identity and cultural diversity
		b) Land of the free?	1.5 Significance; 1.6c Interpretations	3i	
		c) Storming of the Bastille	1.4 Cause/consequence	3i	
		d) Liberty, equality and fraternity	1.5 Significance; 1.6c Interpretations	3i	
		e) Taking it further!: Toussiant L'Ouverture: the hero of Haiti?	1.6a, b, c Interpretations; 2.2a, b Evidence	3i	

Enquiry	Chronological focus	Lessons	Key concepts and processes	Content	Cross-curriculum dimensions
1.6 Why are the people protesting?	1780–1820	a) The Gordon Riots of 1780	1.4 Cause/consequence; 2.1a, 2.1b Enquiry; 2.3b Communicating	3d	Community participation
		b) The Peterloo Massacre	1.6a Interpretation; 2.2b Evidence; 2.3a Communicating	3d	
		c) Taking it further!: The Cato Street Conspiracy	1.4a Cause/consequence; 2.1b Enquiry; 2.3b Communicating	3d	
1.7 Who wanted the vote?	19th century	a) Why did people become Chartists?	2.1a Enquiry	3d	Community participation
		b) Chartism: the ups and downs	2.2a Evidence	3d	Identity and cultural diversity
		c) Taking it further!: Who was Lydia Becker	2.3a, b Communicating	3d	Identity and cultural diversity
1.8 Making connections	Across the period	Who held power between 1603 and 1901?	1.3a Change/continuity	3d	Does not apply
1.9 Assessment 1	17th century	Charles I: martyr or tyrant?	1.6a, b, c Interpretations; 2.2a, b Evidence	3d	
1.10 Assessment 2	Across the period	Was revolution the road to freedom?	1.5 Significance	3d	
Unit 2 Living and working					
2.1 What frightened people in the seventeenth century?	17th century	a) Deadly diseases	1.2 Diversity; 2.2a Evidence	3g	Identity and cultural diversity
		b) Why were people accused of witchcraft	1.2 Diversity; 1.4 Cause/consequence	3g	
		c) Taking it further!: Great Fire of London: accident or arson?	1.6c Interpretations; 2.1a, b Enquiry; 2.2a, b Evidence	3g	
2.2 What was life like for immigrants	18th – 19th centuries	a) Huguenot and Jewish communities	1.2a Diversity; 1.3 Change/continuity	3f, 3g	Identity and cultural diversity

Enquiry	Chronological focus	Lessons	Key concepts and processes	Content	Cross-curriculum dimensions
in Britain?		b) Free black communities in eighteenth- and nineteenth-century Britain	1.2a Diversity, 2.2a Evidence	3f, 3g	
		c) Taking it further!: Mary Seacole and the Crimean War	1.2 Diversity	3f, 3g	Global dimension
2.3 Was the Qing Dynasty educated, cultured and equal?		a) Qing Dynasty homes	2.2a Evidence	3i	
		b) The life of a Qing Dynasty woman	1.2 Diversity	3i	Cultural diversity
2.4 Why did the American Indians move west?	18th – 19th centuries	a) Who were the Seminole?	1.2a Diversity; 1.1c Chronology; 2.2a Evidence	3i	
		b) Black Seminoles	1.2a Diversity; 2.2b Evidence	3i	
		c) Andrew Jackson: hero or villain?	1.5a Significance; 2.1a, 2.1b Enquiry	3i	
		d) What was the 'Trail of Tears'?	1.4a Cause/consequence; 1.5 Significance; 2.2b Evidence; 2.3a Communicating	3i	
2.5 How did British industry change with new technology?	18th – 19th centuries	a) The significance of the steam engine	1.5 Significance	3g	Technology
		b) Reactions to the new technology	1.4 Cause/consequence; 2.2b Evidence	3g	
		c) The cost to women	1.6c Interpretation	3g	
		d) The 'Great Exhibition': did everyone agree?	1.6c Interpretation; 2.2b Evidence	3g, h	
2.6 What was it like to be poor in nineteenth-century Britain?	19th century	a) Life in the workhouse	1.2 Diversity; 2.2a Evidence	3g	Identity and cultural diversity
		b) Poor children	1.3 Change/continuity; 2.2a Evidence	3g	

Enquiry	Chronological focus	Lessons	Key concepts and processes	Content	Cross-curriculum dimensions
2.7 How did urban life change in the nineteenth century?	19th century	a) Growth of the cities	1.3 Change/continuity	3g	Identity and cultural diversity
		b) Public health	1.2 Diversity; 1.3 Change/continuity	3g	Healthy lifestyles
		c) Life in nineteenth-century London	1.3 Change/continuity; 2.3a, b Communicating	3g	Technology
		d) Taking it further!: How did urban life change?	1.5 Significance; 2.2b Evidence; 2.3b Communicating	3g	
2.8 What was law and order like during the eighteenth and nineteenth centuries?	18th – 19th centuries	a) Law and order: how it changed	1.1b Chronology; 2.3b Communicating	3d, 3g	Community participation
		b) Britain's first policemen: were they popular?	2.1a, b Enquiry	3d, 3g	
		c) Taking it further!: Catching Jack the Ripper!	2.1a Enquiry, 2.3a Communicating	3g	
2.9 Making connections	Across the period	Country swap	1.2a Diversity; 2.3a, b Communicating	3i	Creative
2.10 Assessment 1	Across the period	What were the most important changes in living conditions in Britain between 1603 and 1900?	1.3 Change/continuity; 2.3 Communicating	3g	Creative
2.11 Assessment 2	19th century	Were pauper apprentices in nineteenth-century factories all treated the same?	1.5a Significance; 1.6b Interpretation	3g	N/A
Unit 3 Moving and travelling					
3.1 What were the real reasons Britain wanted an empire?	18th – 19th centuries	a) Building the empire	1.4 Cause/consequence	3h	Identity and cultural diversity / Global dimension
3.2 What was slavery?	18th – 19th centuries	a) 'A fine business': slavery as a business venture	1.1c Chronology; 1.4 Cause/consequence; 2.2a Evidence	3h	Identity and cultural diversity
		b) Slave conditions	1.2 Diversity; 2.2b Using evidence;	3h	Global dimension

Enquiry	Chronological focus	Lessons	Key concepts and processes	Content	Cross-curriculum dimensions
			2.3a Communicating		
		c) Did slavery transform Britain?	1.1b Chronology; 2.1a Enquiry; 2.3b Communicating	3h	
		d) Abolition	1.4 Cause/consequence; 2.1b Enquiry	3h	
		e) Taking it further!: How has slavery been interpreted?	1.6a Interpretation; 2.3b Communicating	3h	
3.3 Assessment 1	18th – 19th centuries	What were the arguments for and against slavery?	1.6c Interpretation; 2.2b Evidence; 2.3a Communicating	3h	Identity and cultural diversity Global dimension
3.4 Why did people go exploring?	18th – 19th centuries	a) Cook's voyages of discovery	1.5 Significance	3h	Global dimension; Identity and cultural diversity
		b) An Arctic mystery	1.6c Interpretation; 2.2a, b Evidence	3h	
3.5 Who had to leave?	18th – 19th centuries	a) The Irish Famine: escape to Liverpool	2.2a Evidence; 2.3b Communicating	3e, 3f	Identity and cultural diversity
		b) The Highland Clearances	1.4a Cause/consequence	3e, 3f	
		c) Taking it further!: Remembering the Highland Clearances	2.1a, b Enquiry; 2.2b Evidence	3e, 3f	
3.6 What was the impact of steam on transport?	18th – 19th centuries	a) Life at sea	1.6c Interpretation	3h; 3i	Global dimension
		b) Steam ships	1.3 Change/continuity; 1.5 Significance	3h; 3i	Technology
		c) Why the railways?	1.1c Chronology; 1.3a Change/continuity; 2.3b Communicating	3g	
		d) Impact of the railways	1.5 Significance; 2.2a Evidence	3g	
3.7 What was the British Empire?	18th – 19th centuries	a) Jewel in the crown: a very British India?	2.2a, b Evidence	3h	Global dimension Identity and

Enquiry	Chronological focus	Lessons	Key concepts and processes	Content	Cross-curriculum dimensions
		b) The bullet that started a 'mutiny'	1.4 Cause/consequence; 1.6c Interpretation	3h	cultural diversity
		c) The scramble for Africa	1.1b Chronological understanding;	3h	
		d) Taking it further!: A heroic death?	1.6a,b,c Interpretations; 2.2a,b Using Evidence; 2.1b Enquiry	3i	
3.8 Making connections	Across the period	Why did the ability of people to move and travel change the way they lived?	1.1b Chronological understanding; 1.4 Cause/consequence; 2.2a Evidence; 2.3b Communicating	3f	Creative
3.9 Assessment 2	Across the period	How had travel changed the world by 1901?	1.1a Chronology; 1.5a Significance; 2.2b Evidence; 2.3b Communicating	3f	Global dimension

How to put your Scheme of Work together using *History in Progress* – *Book 2*

On pages 12–17 we have provided an overview of the whole of *History in Progress – Book 2*, allowing you to select the topics you want to teach and ensuring you have full coverage of all the requirements of the new Programme of Study. Below and on the next few pages are four suggestions for how *History in Progress – Book 2* might be incorporated into your Scheme of Work.

Suggestion 1: Teaching Key Stage 3 History in 39 weeks/lessons

Enquiry	Lessons	Key concepts/processes	Content
1.1 What was the English Civil War?	1.1a, b, c	1.2 Diversity; 1.4 Cause/consequence; 1.6c Interpretations; 2.2a, b Evidence	3d, g
1.9 Assessment 1 Unit 1	1.9	1.6a, b, c Interpretations; 2.2a, b Evidence	3d
1.2 Who should be in charge?	1.2a, b	1.3 Change/continuity; 1.6c Interpretations; 2.1a, b Enquiry; 2.2a, b Evidence	3d, g
1.3 Scotland and England: a popular union?	1.3a, b	1.6c Interpretations; 2.2a,b Evidence	3e
1.5 Who wanted their liberty and why?	1.5c, d	1.5 Significance; 1.6a, b, c Interpretations; 2.2a, b Evidence	3e
1.7 Who wanted the vote?	1.7a, b	2.1a Enquiry; 2.2a Evidence	3d
1.10 Assessment 2 Unit 1	1.10	1.5 Significance	3d
1.4 The Chinese Qing: a forgotten empire?	1.4a, b	2.2a, b Evidence; 1.5 Significance	3h, i
2.3 Was the Qing Dynasty educated, cultured and equal?	2.3a, b	2.2a Evidence; 1.2 Diversity	3i
2.2 What was life like for immigrants in Britain?	2.2a, b	1.2a Diversity; 1.3 Change/continuity; 2.2a Evidence	3f, g
2.4 Why did the American Indians move west?	2.4a, b, c, d	1.2a Diversity; 1.1c Chronology; 1.4a Cause/consequence; 1.5 Significance; 2.1a, 2.1b Enquiry; 2.2a, b Evidence; 2.3a Communicating	3i

Enquiry	Lessons	Key concepts/processes	Content
2.5 How did British industry change with new technology?	2.5a, b, c	1.4 Cause/consequence; 1.5 Significance; 1.6c Interpretation; 2.2b Evidence	3g
2.10 Assessment 1 Unit 2	2.10	1.3 Change/continuity; 2.3 Communicating	3g
2.7 How did urban life change in the nineteenth century?	2.7a, b, c	1.2 Diversity; 1.3 Change/continuity; 2.3a, b Communicating	3g
2.11 Assessment 2 Unit 2	2.10	1.5a Significance; 1.6b Interpretation	3g
3.2 What was slavery?	3.2a, b, c, d	1.1b, c Chronology; 1.2 Diversity; 1.4 Cause/consequence; 2.1a, b Enquiry; 2.2a, b Evidence; 2.3a, b Communicating	3h
3.3 Assessment 1 Unit 3	3.3	1.6c Interpretation; 2.2b Evidence; 2.3a Communicating	3h
3.4 Why did people go exploring?	3.4a, b	1.5 Significance; 1.6c Interpretation; 2.2a, b Evidence	3h
3.7 What was the British Empire?	3.7a, b, c	1.1b Chronological understanding; 1.4 Cause/consequence; 1.6a, b, c Interpretation; 2.2a,b Using Evidence; 2.1b Enquiry	3h
3.9 Assessment 2 Unit 3	3.9	1.1a Chronology; 1.5a Significance; 2.2b Evidence; 2.3b Communicating	3f

Suggestion 2: Teaching Key Stage 3 History in 26 weeks

Enquiry	Lessons	Key concepts/processes	Content
1.1 What was the English Civil War?	1.1a, b, c	1.2 Diversity; 1.4 Cause/consequence; 1.6c Interpretations; 2.2a, b Evidence	3d, g
1.3 Scotland and England: a popular union?	1.3a, b	1.6c Interpretations; 2.2a,b Evidence	3e
1.9 Assessment 1 Unit 1	1.9	1.6a, b, c Interpretations; 2.2a, b Evidence	3d
2.2 What was life like for immigrants in Britain?	2.2a, b	1.2a Diversity; 1.3 Change/continuity; 2.2a Evidence	3f, g
2.3 Was the Qing Dynasty educated, cultured and equal?	2.3a, b	2.2a Evidence; 1.2 Diversity	3i
1.5 Who wanted their liberty and why?	1.5a, b, c, d	1.5 Significance; 1.6a, b, c Interpretations; 2.2a, b Evidence	3e
1.7 Who wanted the vote?	1.7a, b	2.1a Enquiry; 2.2a Evidence	3d
1.10 Assessment 2 Unit 1	1.10	1.3 Change/continuity; 2.3 Communicating	3g
2.5 How did British industry change with new technology?	2.5a, b, c	1.4 Cause/consequence; 1.5 Significance; 1.6c Interpretation; 2.2b Evidence	3g

Enquiry	Lessons	Key concepts/processes	Content
2.7 How did urban life change in the nineteenth century?	2.7a, 2.7b	1.2 Diversity; 1.3 Change/continuity; 2.3a, b Communicating	3g
3.1 What were the real reasons Britain wanted an empire?	3.1a	1.4 Cause/consequence	3h
3.2 What was slavery?	3.2a, b, d	1.1 c Chronology; 1.2 Diversity; 1.4 Cause/consequence; 2.1 b Enquiry; 2.2a, b Evidence; 2.3a Communicating	3h
3.3 Assessment 1 Unit 3	3.3	1.6c Interpretation; 2.2b Evidence; 2.3a Communicating	3h
3.7 What was the British Empire?	3.7a, b, c	1.1b Chronological understanding; 1.4 Cause/consequence; 1.6a, b, c Interpretation; 2.2a,b Using Evidence; 2.1b Enquiry	3h

Suggestion 3: A chronological approach to Key Stage 3 History – a 39-week/lesson scheme for Year 8

Enquiry	Lessons	Key concepts/processes	Content
1.1 What was the English Civil War?	1.1a, b, c, d	1.2 Diversity; 1.4 Cause/consequence; 1.6c Interpretations; 2.2a, b Evidence	3d, g
2.1 What frightened people in the seventeenth century?	2.1a, b	1.2 Diversity; 1.4 Cause/consequence; 1.6c Interpretations; 2.1a, b Enquiry; 2.2a, b Evidence	3g
1.3 Scotland and England: a popular union?	1.3a, b	1.6c Interpretations; 2.2a,b Evidence	3e
3.5 Who had to leave?	3.5b	1.4a Cause/consequence	3e, 3f
1.5 Who wanted their liberty and why?	1.5a, b	1.4 Cause/consequence; 1.5 Significance; 1.6c Interpretations	3i
1.9 Assessment 1 Unit 1	1.9	1.6a, b, c Interpretations; 2.2a, b Evidence	3d
2.2 What was life like for immigrants in Britain?	2.2a, b	1.2a Diversity; 1.3 Change/continuity; 2.2a Evidence	3f, g
2.4 Why did the American Indians move west?	2.4a, b, c, d	1.2a Diversity; 1.1c Chronology; 1.4a Cause/consequence; 1.5 Significance; 2.1a, 2.1b Enquiry; 2.2a, b Evidence; 2.3a Communicating	3i
3.2 What was slavery?	3.2a, b, d	1.1 c Chronology; 1.2 Diversity; 1.4 Cause/consequence; 2.1 b Enquiry; 2.2a, b Evidence; 2.3a Communicating	3h
3.3 Assessment 1 Unit 3	3.3	1.6c Interpretation; 2.2b Evidence; 2.3a Communicating	3h
2.5 How did British industry change with new technology?	2.5a, b, c	1.4 Cause/consequence; 1.5 Significance; 1.6c Interpretation; 2.2b Evidence	3g
3.6 What was the impact of steam on transport?	3.6c, d	1.1c Chronology; 1.3a Change/continuity; 1.5 Significance; 2.2a Evidence; 2.3b Communicating	3g

Enquiry	Lessons	Key concepts/processes	Content
3.7 What was the British Empire?	3.7a, b, c	1.1b Chronological understanding; 1.4 Cause/consequence; 1.6a, b, c Interpretation; 2.2a,b Using Evidence; 2.1b Enquiry	3h
2.8 What was law and order like during the eighteenth and nineteenth centuries?	2.8a, b	1.1b Chronology; 2.1a, b Enquiry; 2.3b Communicating	3d, g
2.6 What was it like to be poor in nineteenth-century Britain?	2.6a, b	1.2 Diversity; 1.3 Change/continuity; 2.2a Evidence	3g
2.7 How did urban life change in the nineteenth century?	2.7a, b	1.2 Diversity; 1.3 Change/continuity; 2.3a, b Communicating	3g
1.7 Who wanted the vote?	1.7a, b	2.1a Enquiry; 2.2a Evidence	3d
2.10 Assessment 1 Unit 2	2.10	1.3 Change/continuity; 2.3 Communicating	3g

Suggestion 4: Approaches matched to content of Programme of Study – a 39-week/lesson scheme for Year 8

Enquiry	Lessons	Key concepts/processes	Content
3d) Development of political power			
1.1 What was the English Civil War?	4	1.2 Diversity; 1.4 Cause/consequence; 1.6c Interpretations; 2.2a, b Evidence	3d, g
1.6 Why are the people protesting?	2	1.4 Cause/consequence; 1.6a Interpretation; 2.1a, 2.1b Enquiry; 2.2b Evidence; 2.3a, b Communicating	3d
1.7 Who wanted the vote?	2	2.1a Enquiry; 2.2a Evidence	3d
3e) Changing relationship between England, Scotland and Wales			
1.3 England and Scotland: a popular union?	2	1.6c Interpretations; 2.2a,b Evidence	3e
3.5 Who had to leave?	2	1.4a Cause/consequence; 2.2a Evidence; 2.3b Communicating	3e, 3f
3f) Movement and settlement to, from and within British Isles			
2.2 What was life like for immigrants in Britain?	2	1.2a Diversity; 1.3 Change/continuity; 2.2a Evidence	3f, g
3g) Ways in which the lives, beliefs, ideas and attitudes of people in Britain have changed over time			
2.1 What frightened people in the seventeenth century?	2	1.2 Diversity; 1.4 Cause/consequence; 1.6c Interpretations; 2.1a, b Enquiry; 2.2a, b Evidence	3g
2.7 How did urban life change in the nineteenth century?	2	1.2 Diversity; 1.3 Change/continuity; 2.3a, b Communicating	3g
3h) Development of trade, colonisation, industrialisation and technology, the British Empire and its impact			
2.5 How did British industry change with new technology?	3	1.4 Cause/consequence; 1.5 Significance; 1.6c Interpretation; 2.2b Evidence	3g
3.2 What was slavery?	3	1.1 c Chronology; 1.2 Diversity; 1.4 Cause/consequence; 2.1 b Enquiry; 2.2a, b Evidence; 2.3a Communicating	3h

Enquiry	Lessons	Key concepts/processes	Content
3.4 Why did people go exploring?	2	1.5 Significance; 1.6c Interpretation; 2.2a, b Evidence	3h
3.7 What was the British Empire?	3	1.1b Chronological understanding; 1.4 Cause/consequence; 1.6a, b, c Interpretation; 2.2a,b Using Evidence; 2.1b Enquiry	3h
3i) Impact of political, social, cultural, religious, technological and/or economic developments			
1.4 The Chinese Qing: a forgotten empire?	2	2.2a, b Evidence; 1.5 Significance	3h, i
1.5 Who wanted their liberty and why?	2	1.5 Significance; 1.6a, b, c Interpretations; 2.2a, b Evidence	3e
2.3 Was the Qing Dynasty educated, cultured and equal?	2	2.2a Evidence; 1.2 Diversity	3i
3j) Changing nature of conflict and co-operation			
2.4 Why did the American Indians move west?	4	1.2a Diversity; 1.1c Chronology; 1.4a Cause/consequence; 1.5 Significance; 2.1a, 2.1b Enquiry; 2.2a, b Evidence; 2.3a Communicating	3i

1.1 What was the English Civil War?

1.1a The world turned upside down

Learning objectives
- To discover the main religious and political problems of the seventeenth century.
- To weigh up the greatest problems facing kings in the seventeenth century.

Historical background
This lesson introduces some of the major problems facing the rulers in the seventeenth century which contributed to the outbreak of Civil War in 1642–1648. The religious divisions between Catholics and Protestants were inherited from the sixteenth century but intensified after the gunpowder plot of 1605 which encouraged people to see Catholics as a danger. Political problems for the monarch increased as parliament became more self-assured and desirous of greater independent power which clashed with the monarchy's view of their power as absolute and divinely ordained. It would take considerable skill on the part of the monarch to prevent these issues from flaring up into conflict.

Teaching Activities and Learning Outcomes

Assessment opportunity

Using sources to establish the main religious and political problems in the seventeenth century.

Pupils will be able to

- select relevant information from sources
- prioritise factors for relative importance and be able to justify this in discussion
- explain the main problems facing seventeenth century rulers and justify this with evidence.

Starter

Ask pupils to look at **source a** on page 8 of *History in Progress – Book 2* and think about the questions related to it. The aim of this is to encourage pupils to think about the seventeenth century as a time of change and chaos. Once pupils have identified things that are peculiar about the picture, draw out from them how these are shown in the source, e.g. change and disorder in religion is shown by the upside-down church.

Development

Green task: This task encourages pupils to empathise with a particular character and to interpret evidence from different perspectives according to their character's views. As suggested, this would work well as a paired activity to encourage appreciation of different viewpoints and to encourage discussion. Throughout the enquiries on the seventeenth century pupils will be asked to refer back to the character they created in this lesson, so it is worth them noting down clearly, perhaps as a profile with an illustration, their character for later reference. This can be done using **Worksheet 1.1a**.

Blue task: This develops tasks 1 and 2 and gives opportunities to show comprehension of sources and selection of relevant material. In this task pupils should justify their choices in writing.

Orange task: This develops findings from the earlier tasks; it asks pupils to prioritise the most important problems and justify their choices from the point of view of a seventeenth-century monarch.

Plenary

Pupils suggest what they think was the most serious problem affecting rulers in seventeenth-century England. They share their suggestion with a partner and compare reasons for their ideas.

ICT opportunities

History in Progress – LiveText CD 2: electronic activity

1.1 What was the English Civil War?

Worksheet 1.1a Civil War profile

Use this worksheet to keep a record of the character you are going to select in this lesson. You will need to refer back to what your character might think at various points during this unit. There is also space for you to add an illustration of what your character might look like.

Name: _____

Job: _____

Home town: _____

Church: _____

Three things that most concern your character about religion in England:

_____

_____

_____

Three things that most concern your character about how the country is ruled:

_____

_____

_____

Other notes about your character:

_____

_____

_____

_____

_____

_____

_____

_____

1.1 What was the English Civil War?

1.1b Charles I and the road to war

Learning objectives
- To find out what the disagreements were between King Charles I and Parliament.
- To make a judgement about whether it was Charles I's poor decisions that led to war.

Historical background
King Charles I inherited many problems when he became king in 1625, as was highlighted in the previous lesson. This lesson aims to encourage pupils to understand how far Charles' own actions made the situation worse. Charles became increasingly unpopular with parliament because of his toleration of his Catholic wife's entourage at court which fuelled rumours that he was a secret Catholic, and because of his refusal to share power with parliament, since he remained convinced of his divine right to govern.

Teaching Activities and Learning Outcomes

Assessment opportunity

Understanding causation and appreciating why there might be different opinions about someone's responsibility for an event.

Pupils will be able to

- make decisions about the best options to avoid conflict with parliament
- make a judgement about how sensible Charles' actions were, in comparison with their own decisions
- write persuasive pieces that justify and attack Charles' actions.

Starter

Use **source a** on page 10 of *History in Progress – Book 2* to encourage pupils to think about the division of England into two warring sides, and the types of people who might be on each side.

Development

Green task: Using either their own point of view or the point of view of the character they created in **Lesson 1.1a**, ask pupils to make decisions that they think would prevent war breaking out. **Worksheet 1.1b** provides a template in which to record their answers. Once pupils have done this, inform them of the real decisions Charles made. Use this revelation as the basis for a discussion about whether they think that Charles' actions were wise.

Blue task: In the previous task pupils might have been critical of Charles' decisions; in this task try to encourage them to appreciate why Charles made the decisions he did. Use this task to encourage empathy and for pupils to justify explanations. Try to bring out the fact that kings before Charles also believed in divine right – he was trying to safeguard what he saw as his God-given duty. Also highlight the personal and unprecedented nature of some of parliament's demands, e.g. the demand for Strafford.

Orange task: Pupils design a persuasive propaganda leaflet from the point of view of parliament emphasising that Charles was to blame for the breakdown in relations that led to civil war.

Plenary

Class vote: Should Charles be held personally responsible for the war? Ask two or three pupils to explain why they have voted as they have.

Cross-curricular links

Citizenship: Responsibilities of the ruler to share power and to rule in the best interests of the people.

ICT opportunities

History in Progress – LiveText CD 2: electronic activity

1.1 What was the English Civil War?

Worksheet 1.1b Charles I and the road to war

Fill in the table to show the actions you would have taken for each problem to try to stop war from breaking out. Later your teacher will tell you the real actions Charles took and you can mark these in the appropriate column of your table.

Problem 1, 1637: How should you punish your critics?

Options	Your decision and reasons for this	Charles' real decision
a) Execute them.		
b) Brand them.		
c) Imprison them.		

Problem 2, 1637: After the war, should Charles continue to demand 'Ship Money'?

Options	Your decision and reasons for this	Charles' real decision
a) Ask parliament for permission to collect taxes.		
b) Collect 'Ship Money' without parliament's consent.		
c) Collect 'Ship Money' but reduce the amount.		

Problem 3, 1640: What should the king do?

Options	Your decision and reasons for this	Charles' real decision
a) Reject all of parliament's demands.		
b) Hand over Strafford to parliament.		
c) Refuse to hand over Strafford.		

Problem 4, 1642: What should the king do with the MPs who oppose him?

Options	Your decision and reasons for this	Charles' real decision
a) Agree to parliament's demands.		
b) Arrest the five MPs on their way to the House of Commons.		
c) Arrest the five MPs inside the House of Commons.		

1.1 What was the English Civil War?

1.1c King or parliament?

Learning objectives
- To find out about the Parliamentarians and the Royalists.
- To evaluate sources to understand how propaganda was used by parliament during the Civil War.

Historical background
Civil War broke out in 1642 and lasted until 1648. Ordinary people were forced to make the difficult decision of whether they were for king or parliament. This decision was sometimes made for political or religious reasons, but more often and for most people it was based on where they lived and what side their employer supported. Both sides used propaganda to vilify the enemy to encourage recruits.

Teaching Activities and Learning Outcomes

Assessment opportunities
Evaluating sources for reliability.

Pupils will be able to
- identify key reasons why people decided to fight for the king or parliament
- compare and contrast sources that present different views of the same event
- evaluate sources to establish their reliability.

Starter
Use the map and information on page 12 of *History in Progress – Book* 2 to generate a discussion about the key factors that influenced which side people chose to support. This could also be used as the basis for a discussion about whether these factors gave one side an initial advantage, e.g. the fact that parliament controlled the ports would make it easier for them to get new supplies.

Development
Green task: Pupils use **sources a–c** to establish general impressions of soldiers in the Civil War. Ask pupils to think about who produced the sources to encourage them to question their reliability.

Blue task: Pupils contrast the impression given in **sources d** and **e** about the attack on Cirencester, which encourages them to appreciate how and why one event can be presented in very different ways depending on its origin and purpose. Encourage pupils to think about the 'nature, origin and purpose' formula for evaluating sources. The extracts from the letters of Brilliana Harley (**sources f–h**) on page 15 are designed to build on these skills.

Orange task: Pupils explain how important propaganda was, then give advice on using primary sources to understand about the Royalists in the Civil War. This will encourage them to explain the importance of 'nature, origin and purpose' themselves. It would be worth encouraging pupils to include something about the positives of using primary sources as well, in order to avoid an overly negative response about the 'dangers' of primary sources.

Plenary
What were the Royalists really like? Ask pupils to suggest one thing they can be certain about, one thing they can be fairly sure about and one thing they are not at all sure about, and why. This will help to avoid the belief that because many of the primary sources were not reliable nothing can be learned from them.

Cross-curricular links
Citizenship: Evaluating media stories for reliability and not just accepting propaganda at face value.

ICT opportunities
History in Progress – LiveText CD 2: electronic activity

1.1 What was the English Civil War?

1.1d Eyewitness: Naseby

Learning objectives
- To find out what happened at the Battle of Naseby in 1645.
- To identify, categorise and prioritise causes for parliament's victory at Naseby.

Historical background
The early battles of the Civil War were indecisive. The turning point came with parliament's victory at the Battle of Naseby in 1645. The first phase of the Civil War ended in 1646 when negotiations began with Charles I in custody. However, Charles escaped and encouraged a Scottish invasion of England which opened a second phase in the hostilities. War came to a close in 1648 with parliament's final victory and the imprisonment of Charles I.

Teaching Activities and Learning Outcomes

Assessment opportunity
Identifying, categorising and establishing the relative importance of causal factors.

Pupils will be able to
- identify causes for parliament's victory from an annotated map
- categorise causes for parliament's victory
- write a persuasive explanation to show what they consider to be the most important explanations for parliament's victory.

Starter
Pupils study the map of the Battle of Naseby on page 16 of *History in Progress – Book 2* and generate a list of their impressions of battles in the Civil War. They might focus on the types of weapons used, the tactics of fighting in pitched battles, etc.

Development
Green task: Pupils work in pairs to identify reasons why parliament might have won, using the map annotations. When feeding back in a class discussion, encourage pupils to come up with their own categories in which to group these factors, which will lead on to task 2 focusing on the categories of: leadership, training and skill of troops, effectiveness of recruitment and alliances.

Blue task: A development of task 1, which now focuses on categorising factors. Pupils should complete the table, then give each army a score for each category. **Worksheet 1.1d** supports this activity. Stress to pupils that their score may differ from their partner's, but that this doesn't matter as long as they can justify their score.

Orange task: Use the scores pupils recorded in their tables as a stimulus for discussion about what the most important category was in explaining parliament's victory in the Civil War. Try to encourage pupils to defend their score by explaining it in discussion or to their partner. More able pupils should be encouraged to establish importance by explaining the relative significance of their chosen factor in comparison to another factor.

Plenary
Class vote: What do pupils think was the most important factor in parliament's victory? Pupils should be ready to justify their opinions.

ICT opportunities
History in Progress – LiveText CD 2: electronic activity

1.1 What was the English Civil War?

Worksheet 1.1d Eyewitness: Naseby

Fill in the table below for both the Royalist and Parliamentary armies at the Battle of Naseby in 1645. For each category give each army a score out of 5:

- 5 = excellent
- 0 = hopeless

Make sure you give a reason in each box to explain the score you have awarded.

Category	Royalists	Parliament
Quality of leadership		
Size, training and discipline of troops		
Raising men, money and supplies for their army		
Making useful alliances		

Discuss with a partner or another pair which of the four categories in the table above you think was most important in explaining why parliament won the Civil War. If you disagree with their choice, you need to convince them you are right, so make sure you have evidence to back up your choice.

1.1 What was the English Civil War?

1.1e Taking it further! How to punish a king?

Learning objectives
- To find out the reasons why King Charles I was put on trial and executed in 1649.
- To select evidence to support different arguments and to write a persuasive argument.

Historical background
It was only reluctantly that parliament decided on the necessity of executing Charles in 1649. This extreme position was reached due to the king's failure to negotiate a settlement, his untrustworthiness in having escaped from custody in 1646 and his conduct during the Civil War. But many refused to recognise the legitimacy of parliament placing the king on trial. Indeed, Charles refused to defend himself at the trial claiming it was an illegal trial, since as king by divine right there was no authority on earth with the power to sit in judgement over him. When Charles was executed in January 1649 many were deeply shocked and Charles quickly became revered by many as a martyr king.

Teaching Activities and Learning Outcomes

Assessment opportunity
Selecting evidence in support of an argument; writing in order to persuade.

Pupils will be able to
- select evidence to support different arguments about whether Charles should be executed
- design a persuasive pamphlet setting down the arguments for the necessity of the execution.

Starter
Ask pupils to list some of the possible options that parliament might consider about what to do with Charles I now that parliament had won the Civil War. Their choices might include: imprison him permanently; execute him; exile him; replace him as king with his young son, Charles. Pupils might also discuss the advantages and disadvantages of each option.

Development
- Pupils to choose, or be allocated, one of the three differing points of view (shown in task 1) about what to do with Charles and to select evidence to support their argument. This could be used as the basis for discussion. This discussion could also be held as a class debate or as a mock-up of the trial of Charles himself. A vote or a jury could then decide their verdict.
- Pupils should be able to design a persuasive pamphlet justifying the reasons why parliament did decide to execute the king. Pupils should stress the failure of Charles to compromise, his lack of trustworthiness and his behaviour in the Civil War which added to the suffering of the British people, to explain why he was accused of treason against the state.

Plenary
Encourage pupils to refer back to the character which they created at the start of the enquiry and to decide whether they would have been for or against the execution of the king. Pupils could share their opinions in pairs or in class discussion. Point out that most ordinary people were deeply shocked by the execution of the king.

Cross-curricular links
Citizenship: The responsibility of the ruler to safeguard the rights and freedom of the people, and the consequences for failure to do so.

ICT opportunity
History in Progress – LiveText CD 2: electronic activity

© Pearson Education Ltd 2008: *History in Progress – Planning and Resource Pack 2*

1.1 What was the English Civil War?

Worksheet 1.1e What should happen to Charles I?

1 Imagine you have been asked to represent one group of MPs. You can select from the following.

- Radical/Puritan MPs: they want to execute the king.
- Moderate MPs: they want to remove Charles but keep a monarchy.
- Royalist sympathiser MPs: they want to reinstate the king.

Which evidence would you select to make your case for what should happen to Charles?

2 Once you have selected your evidence, think about what your opponents might say. How will you respond to their arguments?

The Civil war was Charles' fault. He made a deal with the Scots to invade England in 1648.

There are still many Royalists in England who might stir up rebellion and try to put the king back on the throne.

Charles escaped from prison in 1647. He might try again.

Charles ruled badly, taxing the people heavily and refusing to take advice from parliament.

Charles declared war on parliament in 1642.

Charles tried to get help from Holland and other foreign rulers during the Civil War.

Charles believes that he is king by divine right, and that it would be wrong for him to give any of his God-given power to parliament.

Parliament has been trying for years to make a deal with Charles I to share power more fairly. He always refuses.

Parliament has become power-hungry. Who's to say it will do any better than the king?

Other monarchs in Europe might invade England to help Charles.

God will punish those who kill a king who is ruler by divine right.

Parliament pushed Charles into declaring war in the first place by making unreasonable demands.

According to the law the king is the most powerful judge in England, so it is illegal for parliament to put a king on trial and judge him.

Charles' eldest son, also called Charles, is 19 years old and living in France. Although he fought for his father in the early years of the Civil War, we know little about his personality or political beliefs.

1.2 Who should be in charge?

1.2a Parliament or king?

Learning objectives
- To use sources to find out about the nature of the rule of Oliver Cromwell and Charles II.
- To make a judgement about the benefits and disadvantages of the rule of each.

Historical background
Cromwell ruled England as Lord Protector after the execution of Charles I until his death in 1658, during the only period in history when England did not have a monarch. Cromwell's rule provokes very different reactions. To some he was a tyrant who unlawfully executed a king, ruled through military might and treated his enemies with cruelty, most notoriously in the massacre of Catholics at Drogheda in Ireland. However, to others he tried to rule in the best interests of the people, championed parliamentary power and exercised a religious toleration rare at the time. After his death, England was briefly ruled by his son Richard Cromwell (although he proved unsuited to the role), and Charles II, son of Charles I, was invited back to rule by the army. Charles II's return was marked by celebrations throughout England.

Teaching Activities and Learning Outcomes

Assessment opportunities

Making judgements using sources as evidence.

Pupils will be able to

- use sources to make a judgement about life during the rules of Cromwell and Charles II
- write an explanation of the positive and negative features of the rule of Cromwell and Charles II.

Starter

Pupils look at **sources a** and **b** on pages 20 of *History in Progress – Book 2* and make suggestions about what impression these portraits give. Pupils might focus on the glamour of Charles II versus the plainness of Oliver Cromwell, or that Charles II is shown at his coronation, whereas Cromwell doesn't seem to be a king. Use the sources to generate discussion about what their personalities might be like, e.g. Cromwell's religious austerity; Charles II's taste in clothes and women!

Development

Green task: Pupils use **sources c–h** to rate each ruler from the point of view of the character they created in the **Lesson 1.1a**. If pupils cannot remember their character, the tasks could be undertaken from their own point of view. Alternatively, you could provide a character, e.g.: a Catholic landowner who supported the Royalists in the Civil War; a Protestant farm worker who was neutral in the Civil War; a Puritan trader who fought for parliament in the Civil War. **Worksheet 1.2a** supports this task.

Blue task: This develops task 1 and asks pupils to make a decision about which ruler they/their character would have preferred to live under. (**Worksheet 1.2a** can be used for this.) Encourage pupils to prioritise categories and to justify why one category is most important in making an overall decision. This task is best preceded by a class or pairs discussion, as this will help to clarify their explanations.

Orange task: This task provides the opportunity for more extended and empathetic writing.

Plenary

Return to **sources a** and **b** used in the **starter**. Now pupils have found out more about each ruler do they think these portraits offer fair reflections of the qualities of each and nature of their rule? Why? Why not?

ICT opportunity

History in Progress – LiveText CD 2: electronic activity

1.2 Who should be in charge?

Worksheet 1.2a Parliament or king?

Read **sources c–h** on pages 20-21 of *History in Progress – Book 2*. As either yourself or the character you created in **Lesson 1.1a** mark Oliver Cromwell and Charles II out of 10 for each category.

- 10 = you are very pleased with their rule
- 0 = you are very displeased with their rule

Remember to give a reason in each box to justify the score you have given.

	Oliver Cromwell	**Charles II**
Religious freedom		
Fun, entertainment and leisure		
Having your say (representation and parliament)		
Law and order		
Personality of the ruler		

Which ruler would your character have preferred to live under? Remember that some issues might be more important to your character than others. Give reasons for your character's preferred ruler.

_____

_____

_____

_____

1.2 Who should be in charge?

1.2b England invaded!

Learning objectives
- To find out what happened in 1688 when William of Orange claimed the throne.
- To use sources as evidence to judge whether William's claim to the throne was popular.

Historical background
The Glorious Revolution is the name given to the change in monarch and constitution that took place in 1688 when William of Orange replaced James II as ruler of England. William of Orange was married to Mary, daughter of James II, and William was invited by parliament to become monarch when parliament felt it could no longer work with James II, whose repeated refusal to take advice from parliament and insistent favouring of Catholics had alienated parliament. William was a Protestant and agreed to certain limitations on his power as king when he became monarch, which made for a much more harmonious relationship with parliament. However, real authority was still exercised by the king.

Teaching Activities and Learning Outcomes

Homework
Use ICT to produce a newspaper article account of why William claimed the throne in 1688.

Pupils will be able to
- select evidence from sources
- understand the reasons why William III claimed the throne in 1688
- write an explanation of the reasons for 1688, showing an awareness of different points of view of the event.

Starter
Pupils generate a list of questions they would like to ask if they arrived at the scene of William's landing in Devon. The list might include questions such as: How many troops does William have? Why is he claiming the throne? Is it an invasion? What are his chances of success?

Development
Green task: Pupils formalise and choose questions they wish to ask. They should aim for about four questions each. They then use the sources on pages 22-23 of History in Progress – Book 2 to find answers to their questions. The story board task asks pupils to order their work under key headings.

Blue task: As a development of tasks 1 and 2 and in preparation for task 4 pupils write a dialogue for an interview with one of the witnesses used in the sources. More able pupils should be encouraged to challenge the reliability of the witnesses during the interview.

Orange task: This provides pupils with the opportunity to write a newspaper explanation for why William III claimed the throne in 1688. More able pupils should be encouraged to write a persuasive piece in support of or against William III.

Plenary
Think, pair, share: Pupils draw conclusions about whether they think the coming of William III will improve or worsen the way England is governed.

ICT opportunity
History in Progress – LiveText CD 2: electronic activity

1.3 Scotland and England: a popular union?

1.3a Were the Scottish MPs bribed?

Learning objectives
- To find out the reasons for and against a union between England and Scotland in 1707.
- To make a judgement about how far the union with England was to the advantage of Scotland.

Historical background
England and Scotland had been united by the same monarch since 1603 when James VI of Scotland became James I of England. It was at this time that the basic design of the Union flag was made though the countries remained separate in all other ways with different laws, legal systems, parliaments and Church. In 1707 the Act of Union made for a more thorough union. Scotland lost its separate parliament but sent representatives to Westminster (this has been partially reversed since devolution in 1999). The main consensus about how far Scotland gained from the union is that although political independence was lost, the economic benefits of the union were very important for Scotland.

Teaching Activities and Learning Outcomes

Homework
Use the Back to the start activity as homework. Pupils could prepare notes either for or against a separate Scottish Parliament to contribute to a debate at the start of the next lesson.

Pupils will be able to
- select evidence to support rival arguments, for and against union between England and Scotland
- understand the importance of the reliability of sources in how far their evidence can be believed
- write a persuasive account using sources as evidence in support of the union.

Starter
Worksheet 1.3a: pupils sort statements for and against the union or according to point of view: English or Scottish. Use as a basis for discussion in which reasons are categorised, e.g. into military, economic, religious and political reasons. Do the pupils think that one of these factors will be more decisive?

Development
Green task: Pupils discuss and then generate a list of questions they would ask one of the MPs accused of bribery, e.g.: Why did you suddenly change your mind about the union? Was the bribe enough money to make you change your mind? Did you support the union even before you were offered money? Is there another reason why you took money from the British?

Blue task: Pupils use relevant information from the evidence listed on pages 24-25 of *History in Progress – Book 2* to write a complaint to one of the Scottish MPs who has been accused of bribery, setting out why they think the union would be a bad thing.

Orange task: Pupils write a response from one of the MPs, explaining why they think the union with England was a good thing.

Plenary
Group discussion: Pupils discuss whether they think the union between England and Scotland was most beneficial to one or both countries. Perhaps introduce the pupils to recent developments in devolved government; do they think this is a good idea?

Cross-curricular links
Citizenship: Links to devolved power to a Scottish Parliament in 1999.

ICT opportunity
History in Progress – LiveText CD 2: electronic activity

1.3 Scotland and England: a popular union?

Worksheet 1.3a Reasons for and against the union

Read through the statements below.

- Which do you think argue in favour of a union between England and Scotland?
- Which argue against it?
- Which show a Scottish point of view and which show an English point of view?

Scotland will lose independence. England will be making decisions on Scotland's behalf.

England has a large army so Scotland will be more secure.

Scottish merchants will be able to trade on equal terms with countries in England's empire.

The Anglican Church in England might not accept the Scottish Presbyterian Church.

Scotland and France have often been allies in the past. It could be disastrous for England if this happened again.

Many English merchants do not want to share their trading rights with the Scots.

Protestant Scottish lowlanders dislike the Scottish Catholic highlanders more than they dislike the English. They feel threatened by the Highlanders.

England wants to have only Protestant kings and queens. There is the possibility that the Scots might choose a Catholic king.

1.3 Scotland and England: a popular union?

1.3b Was Bonnie Prince Charlie brave or foolish?

Learning objectives
- To find out what happened when Bonnie Prince Charlie attempted to claim the throne in 1745.
- To make a judgement about whether Bonnie Prince Charlie was brave or foolish.

Historical background
Ever since James II was removed as monarch in 1688 and replaced by William of Orange in the Glorious Revolution, some British people continued to acknowledge the descendents of James II's son, James Stuart, as rightful monarchs of England. These supporters of the descendents of James Stuart (including Bonnie Prince Charlie) were known as Jacobites. There were several Jacobite-inspired uprisings, but the most serious was led by Bonnie Prince Charlie in 1745, when his supporters, mostly from the Scottish highlands, reached Derby in an attempt to take the throne from King George II. However, the uprising failed and although Bonnie Prince Charlie has been romanticised as the boy who should have been king, the failure of the uprising was partly due to his mistakes.

Teaching Activities and Learning Outcomes

Assessment opportunity
Using evidence to evaluate the merits of differing interpretations of Bonnie Prince Charlie.

Pupils will be able to
- select information from the map in order to justify different interpretations of Bonnie Prince Charlie
- write an obituary for Bonnie Prince Charlie to explain their interpretation of his as brave or foolish
- use evidence to support their conclusions in a piece of extended writing.

Starter
Pupils use the family tree on page 26 of *History in Progress – Book 2* to judge who they think had the best claim to the throne. Remind them of the Glorious Revolution when James II was removed from the throne for religious and political reasons to explain why Bonnie Prince Charlie's claim to the throne was overlooked.

Development
Green task: Pupils make suggestions about what Bonnie Prince Charlie was like based on **source a** on page 26. Pupils might mention: youthfulness, Scottish, proud, cheerful. Perceptions could perhaps be challenged by emphasising this is the propaganda image and that the reality might be different.

Blue task: Pupils select appropriate evidence from the annotated map in support of both interpretations of Bonnie Prince Charlie. Use this as the basis for discussion.

Orange task: This develops task 2 and provides the opportunity for pupils to provide an extended persuasive piece of writing in the form of an obituary to support the interpretation of Bonnie Prince Charlie they most agree with. More able pupils should be encouraged to synthesise the interpretation from task 2 to develop their own argument.

Plenary
Back to the start: Allow pupils 5 minutes to discuss this in pairs, then take feedback.

Cross-curricular links
Citizenship: Discussion of the merits of devolved government for Scotland, in operation since 1999.

ICT opportunities
History in Progress – LiveText CD 2: electronic activity

1.4 The Chinese Qing: a forgotten empire?

1.4a China: the 'Middle Kingdom'

Learning objectives
- To investigate Lord Macartney's visit to China.
- To compare the concept of Empire of the Chinese Qing Dynasty and the British Empire.

Historical background
During the Qing Dynasty Taiwan, Chinese Central Asia, Mongolia and Tibet were all attached to China. The population grew rapidly and by 1850 China had a population of over 400 million. China felt it did not have to trade with the rest of the world as it had all it would ever need. It felt foreign nations were inferior and should be kept away as they would infect China with Western ways.

Teaching Activities and Learning Outcomes

Assessment opportunity

Task 4 Cultural diversity, comparing the Chinese concept of Empire with the British concept.

Pupils will be able to

- write a letter or postcard describing Macartney's journey to and arrival in China
- use a pictorial source to assess the significance of the refusal of Macartney to kowtow
- use Emperor Qianlong's letter of response to King George III to establish why the mission failed.

Starter

Pupils use the map on **Worksheet 1.4a** to describe the growth of the Qing Empire. The map shows areas discussed in the lesson along with an overview of the expansion during the period and the development of an Empire. More able pupils will be able to see the significance of Chinese growth to the development of the British Empire with particular reference to British India.

Development

- **Green task:** Pupils should be able to describe the awe and wonder of the British and Chinese at the sight of each other. More able pupils may be able to display the fire this ignited in young Staunton and, in the postcard, talk about his future ambitions in the area.
- **Blue task:** Pupils should explain how performance of the kowtow would be viewed personally and politically. More able pupils should begin to examine how this is the meeting of two empires and how their imperialistic views are clashing. They should be able to relate the significance of this to the close proximity of the empires identified in the starter.
- **Orange task:** Pupils evaluate the real causes of the failure of the mission. Although at first glance it may seem to have been the reluctance of Macartney to kowtow, the letters reveal it is more about the Chinese concept of empire contrasting directly with Britain's expansionist policies.

Plenary

Pupils vote as to whether British and Chinese actions were justified. Half the class should vote from a Chinese point of view and the other half from a British point of view. Both groups should explain their answers taking into consideration the imperialistic views of both empires.

Cross-curricular links

Geography, Citizenship.

ICT opportunities

Pupils research the Opium trade, the reversal of trade in silver, China and Britain and the Opium War.

History in Progress – LiveText CD 2: electronic activity

Unit 1: The Chinese Qing: a forgotten empire?

Worksheet 1.4a China: the 'Middle Kingdom'

Use the map below to describe the growth of the Qing Empire to a partner. Use dates and names of places. Look particularly at blocks of power being created.

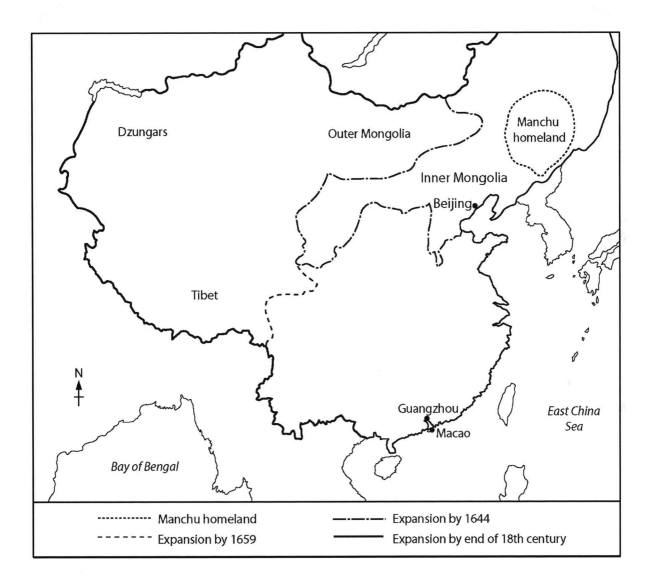

1.4 The Chinese Qing: a forgotten empire?

1.4b How was China ruled?

Learning objectives
- To investigate the government and bureaucracy of Qing Dynasty China.
- To analyse the significance of the Qing system of governance for those who lived under it.

Historical background
The Qing system of governance was ordered and all positions were shared by a Han and a Manchu. This helped to foster acceptance of the invading forces and created civil harmony for a while. Dependency on an absolute ruler did create issues particularly in the failing years of Emperor Qianlong. The growth of the Chinese Empire and its growing trading relations with European powers also created issues that this outmoded style of government could not cope with.

Teaching Activities and Learning Outcomes

Assessment opportunity

Tasks 2 and 3: Analyse the significance of the Qing system of governance for those who lived under it.

Pupils will be able to

- create a flowchart or diagram to illustrate the Qing system of government
- analyse the system of crime and punishment
- analyse modern interpretations of the Qing system of government and evaluate its effectiveness.

Starter

After answering the opening question on page 30, pupils then use **Worksheet 1.4b** to describe what impression the Emperor is trying to portray. This activity gives pupils the opportunity to appreciate how an invading force must maintain the image of a strong force where subordination and rebellion will not be tolerated. This links well with the reasons why such stringent systems of government were introduced.

Development

- **Green task:** Pupils gain an overview of the control the Qing Emperor had on all aspects of life, and by ordering their description in a flow chart it will illustrate how ordered the system actually was.
- **Blue task:** Pupils examine the advantages and disadvantages of the Legal Code as one example of the work of a Board. The system appears ordered but there are so many considerations, and the officials under such a threat themselves, that it would be difficult to judge the system as fair.
- **Orange task:** Pupils should be able to relate issues with the government of the Empire to the organisation of the system, focusing on the key role the Emperor played and how vital it was they were effective. Pupils should discuss the problems associated with the growth of the empire and the growth of trade with Europe relating all three activities together. Pupils will also consider why officials at the time would not have pointed out the flaws in the system.

Plenary

Pupils answer three questions: What did you already know at the start of the lesson? What have you learned in this lesson? What else do you need to know?

Cross-curricular links

Law, Citizenship, Government and politics

ICT opportunities

History in Progress – LiveText CD 2: electronic activity

The Chinese Qing: a forgotten empire

Worksheet 1.4b How was China ruled?

Look carefully at the picture of the Manchu warrior. The Emperor had 100 portraits like this of his bodyguards. They were all hung in the palace hall where state banquets were held.

- Describe the warrior.
- What impression is the Emperor trying to give of the Qing Dynasty to the Chinese and foreign visitors?
- Why is it important to give such an impression?

1.5 Who wanted their liberty and why?

1.5a Yorktown and the end of British North America

Learning objectives
- To understand why the British lost control of America in 1781.
- To identify short- and long-term causes to explain why the British lost control of America.

Historical background
Until the War of Independence in 1775, America was ruled by Britain. However, many Americans increasingly felt their interests were not represented by the British government, especially as taxation was raised without Americans having representation in the British parliament. The refusal of some Americans to pay taxes provoked Britain to increase her military presence in America and the situation degenerated into war. Americans fought for their independence and declared their wish to establish a republican state in which liberty and equality were enshrined in law. The Declaration of Independence certainly seemed to support such principles but in reality liberty and equality was not achieved for all.

Teaching Activities and Learning Outcomes

Assessment opportunity
Identification and categorisation of causes.

Pupils will be able to
- identify the reasons the Americans went to war against the British in 1775
- categorise reasons according to short- and long-term causes
- make a judgement about whether British loss of control of America was inevitable.

Starter
Pupils look at **source a** on page 32 of *History in Progress – Book 2* to decide who they think are the victors and why. Pupils could be asked to consider the differences between the American flag in the painting and the contemporary American flag. In the painting the flag only has 13 stars representing the fact that there were only 13 states at that time, in contrast with the 50 states today.

Development
Green task: Pupils identify the reasons Americans volunteered to fight against the British, then categorise these into short and long term. This could be the basis for discussion, perhaps categorising further to social, economic and political reasons.

Blue task: Pupils work on a persuasive piece from the American perspective against British rule. Encourage them to categorise their reasons in their explanation.

Orange task: Encourage pupils to evaluate the relative importance of short- and long-term factors by asking them to consider whether it was likely that the British would lose control of American at some point anyway. This task would best be preceded by discussion in order to enable pupils to develop their justifications for their thinking. Following this you could ask pupils to think about the importance of Washington to the end of British rule in America. He has been called the 'Father of America'. Would the Revolution have been successful without him? Pupils might consider long-term factors that Washington could not control, the mistakes of the British at Yorktown, and Washington's contribution.

Plenary
3-2-1: Pupils make a note of three things they have learned this lesson, two ways in which they have learned and one thing they need to improve on for next time.

ICT opportunities
History in Progress – LiveText CD 2: electronic activity

1.5 Who wanted their liberty and why?

1.5b Land of the free?

Learning objectives
- To find out how life in America changed after the War of Independence.
- To make a judgement about how far life improved in America after Independence.

Historical background
After America won independence from British rule in the War of Independence, the Bill of Rights stated the fundamental principles on which America would be ruled. America gained a reputation as the 'Land of the Free' and this lesson seeks to explore the extent to which this was justified by looking at the experiences of a cross-section of the American population in the eighteenth century.

Teaching Activities and Learning Outcomes

Assessment opportunity

Using evidence in making judgements and persuasive explanations.

Pupils will be able to

- select information from sources to support different interpretations of life in America after Independence
- make judgements about whose life was changed most by the American Revolution
- write a persuasive argument/brochure on how far life improved in America after the Revolution.

Starter

Think, pair, share: Encourage pupils to think critically about the Bill of Rights (**source a** on page 34 of *History in Progress – Book 2*) through a discussion of what surprises them about its content. Pupils might suggest the right to bear firearms as surprising. They might also recognise as still important today many of its other clauses. The questions on page 35 can be used to start the discussion.

Development

Green task: Pupils select evidence to support the different interpretations about whether life improved for people in America after the Revolution. Use this as the basis for discussion in which pupils decide who benefited most and who benefited least.

Blue task: This is a development of task 1 in which pupils justify, in writing, their ideas from the previous discussion. Pupils should be encouraged to support their views with evidence.

Orange task: This develops tasks 1 and 2 and provides pupils with the opportunity to summarise the main arguments from the lesson about the impact of the American Revolution. Pupils should be encouraged to organise their arguments according to themes, and to include illustrations and interviews in their brochure.

Plenary

Thumbs up!: Having found out more about life after the Revolution, pupils show whether they agree (thumbs up), disagree (thumbs down) or are not sure (thumb in the middle) with the following statements.

- The Bill of Rights meant that life improved for people in America.
- The Bill of Rights meant that for some people in America life improved after the Revolution.

Cross-curricular links

Citizenship: People's fundamental rights.

ICT opportunities

History in Progress – LiveText CD 2: electronic activity

1.5 Who wanted their liberty and why?

1.5c Storming of the Bastille

Learning objectives
- To discover what happened in France on 14 July 1789.
- To categorise reasons to explain why the French stormed the Bastille in 1789.

Historical background
The French Revolution began in July 1789 when Parisians stormed the Bastille (a royal prison) in protest against the unjust rule of King Louis XVI. Parisians particularly resented Louis XVI's power to imprison people without trial, to impose high taxes, to conscript them into the army and his refusal to reform feudalism which forbade peasants to own their own land. French troops had assisted the Americans in their War of Independence, so the ideas of liberty and equality came back to France with the soldiers. As a result of the Revolution, a republican government was established in France.

Teaching Activities and Learning Outcomes

Assessment opportunity
Identifying, categorising and explaining the causes of an event.

Pupils will be able to
- identify the main causes of discontent amongst people in Paris
- categorise the reasons for discontent into long and short term factors
- write an extended explanation for why the French Revolution occurred.

Starter
- Using **source a** (the American Declaration of Independence) on page 36 of *History in Progress – Book 2* pupils make explicit links between the American Revolution and the French Revolution.
- Alternatively pupils use the questions on page 36 to deduce information from **source b**. Make the point that it is not strange for people to want to free prisoners if they think those prisoners are unjustly imprisoned. An attack on the king's prison was viewed as an attack on his authority.

Development
Green task: Pupils identify the main causes of discontent in Paris at the time of the Revolution. Discussion could extend this by focusing on what pupils think were the most serious grievances.

Blue task: Pupils identify political reasons to add to the social and economic reasons for the revolution found in task 1. They should be able to categorise the reasons according to long- and short-term causes.

Orange task: Pupils write an extended piece in the style of an essay (although the task could be adapted to designing a poster for less able pupils) explaining why Parisians stormed the Bastille in 1789. Pupils should plan the essay before they write, organising their ideas into categories such as: long-term and short-term causes; and economic, social and political causes. Encourage more able pupils to make a judgement about the relative importance of these factors in causing the Revolution.

Plenary
Pupils explain to a partner what they think is the most important cause of the French Revolution and why.

Cross-curricular links
Citizenship: The importance of government safeguarding the rights of its citizens.

ICT opportunities
History in Progress – LiveText CD 2: electronic activity

1.5 Who wanted their liberty and why?

1.5d Liberty, equality and fraternity

Learning objectives
- To discover what changes were made in France as a result of the French Revolution.
- To weigh up how far life changed for the better in France as a result of the Revolution.

Historical background
In 1789 a French Republican government was established proclaiming liberty, equality and fraternity for all. But, faced by war with Austria and internal revolts, the Republic became desperate and suspicious. The Terror began from 1792 and thousands of potential opponents were sent to the guillotine, including the king and queen in 1793. It seemed in many ways that the Revolution had betrayed the principles on which it was founded.

Teaching Activities and Learning Outcomes

Assessment opportunity
Making judgements about the significance of an event.

Pupils will be able to
- select evidence from sources to support conclusions about the nature of the French Revolution
- make a judgement about how far the Revolution brought liberty and equality to France
- write a paragraph using evidence to justify their interpretation about the impact of the Revolution.

Starter
Use the questions on page 38 of *History in Progress – Book 2*, which require pupils to think about the continuing importance of the Declaration of the Rights of Man. Pupils might emphasise the importance of having free speech and the importance of the presumption of innocence. They should also think of examples of countries/times when these rights have not been taken for granted.

Development
Green task: Pupils should work in pairs to discuss how far each character benefited from the Revolution. Perhaps pupils could be divided into groups to consider one character and to write an interview with, or profile of, this character to share with the class. This could lead to a discussion focusing on which types of people benefited most and why.

Blue task: Refer pupils back to the starter in which they looked at the Declaration of the Rights of Man. They might highlight that the presumption of innocence doesn't seem to have been the case during The Terror and that freedom of belief isn't entirely allowed since some Catholic churches are closed down, and women and black people are not given equality with white men.

Orange task: This task asks pupils to make a judgement about their interpretation of how beneficial the Revolution was to France. They should justify their opinion with evidence and should be able to categorise their points for clarity, thinking about religious freedom, personal freedom, etc.

Plenary
Discuss as class whether the French Revolution achieved anything and why it is celebrated so much today. Highlight the importance of the ideals it celebrated even if not all of these were achieved.

Cross-curricular links
Citizenship: Fundamental human rights and freedoms.

ICT opportunities
History in Progress – LiveText CD 2: electronic activity

1.5 Who wanted their liberty and why?

1.5e Taking it further!: Toussaint L'Ouverture: the hero of Haiti?

Learning objectives
- To find out about Toussaint L'Ouverture's leadership of the successful slave revolt on Haiti.
- To evaluate the reliability of sources to make a judgement about Toussaint L'Ouverture.

Historical background
In the eighteenth century slavery was seen as an essential part of life on the French-owned Caribbean island of San Domingo where slaves were used to work on the sugar plantations. When, in 1789, the French Revolution declared equality for all, including the abolition of slavery, this triggered the discontented and abused blacks on the island of San Domingo to rebel against their French masters. Their revolt was successful; the island became independent of France and was ruled by former slaves despite Napoleon's attempt to re-impose slavery in 1802. However, the island suffered greatly from the years of war and became isolated and beset by poverty.

Teaching Activities and Learning Outcomes

Assessment opportunity
Evaluating the reliability of sources as evidence in making a conclusion.

Pupils will be able to
- select information from a source
- evaluate the reliability of a source by looking at its nature, origin and purpose
- justify an opinion about Toussaint L'Ouverture, using the sources as evidence.

Starter
Use **source a** on page 40 of *History in Progress – Book 2* to generate an impression of Toussaint.

Development
- **Task 1:** Pupils note for **sources b–h** the overall impression of Toussaint that is given and also how trustworthy the information is. Remind pupils to use the 5Ws when questioning the sources. This could be recorded as a score between 0 and 5. Pupils should be able to justify the score they have given referring to the nature, origin and purpose of the source. **Worksheet 1.5e** supports this activity.
- Pupils will probably be quick to select as unreliable **source g**, since Georges Biassou had personal reasons to portray Toussaint in a negative light.
- More able students will identify CLR James as reliable since as a historian he sought to write an objective account. They might note that the two sources written by him (**sources b** and **e**) taken together present a balanced view of Toussaint, showing positive and negative characteristics.
- Pupils might also cite John Brown (**source f**) as reliable since, even though he was an opponent of slavery, he seems critical of Toussaint's methods.
- **Task 2:** Pupils use the information to decide how far they agree with each claim about Toussaint. Pupils should be encouraged to use the sources as a set to establish greater certainty and to take into account how reliable they believed the source to be when making a decision. Pupils might want to vary the degree of certainty with which they agree or disagree with a statement, and this should be encouraged as long as it can be justified.

Plenary
How far do pupils now think **source a** portrays an accurate impression of Toussaint?

ICT opportunities
History in Progress – LiveText CD 2: electronic activity

1.5 Who wanted their liberty and why?

Worksheet 1.5e Toussaint L'Ouverture: the hero of Haiti?

Use **sources b–h** on pages 40-41 of *History in Progress – Book 2* to find out more about Toussaint to complete the table below. **Watch out!** You need to think carefully about who wrote each of the sources. Use information about the authors to help you with the last two points.

Source	Opinion of Toussaint?	Who wrote it?	Why they wrote it	Reliable? (score 0–5)
B				
C				
D				
E				
F				
G				
H				

1.6 Why are the people protesting?

1.6a The Gordon Riots of 1780

Learning objectives
- To find out why the Gordon Riot started, and what the impact was on London.
- To be able to investigate why a street protest became a riot.

Historical background
With an expanding empire and conflicts with France, Spain and America, the British government of the day needed further military manpower. One source that had been unavailable to them were Catholics, who were subject to many discriminatory laws. Legislation to ease this discrimination and allow them to engage in military service led to opposition from Lord Gordon and the Protestant Association. Their protests lead to widespread rioting and nearly 300 deaths.

Teaching Activities and Learning Outcomes

Assessment opportunity
Identifying the cause and nature of protest; evaluating evidence to identify the consequences of protest.

Pupils will be able to
- sort evidence to reach a conclusion
- identify reasons for a specific protest
- determine key points for protest and examine the differences between motives and outcomes.

Starter
Pupils look at the starter task on 42 of *History in Progress – Book 2*. This activity has the bonus of providing a fully formed list of possible reasons that can be referred to throughout the tasks.

Development
Green task: This sets the scene while developing a sense of chronology. Although a relatively straightforward task, identifying exactly when and why they believe a protest turned into a riot reinforces the starter. Pupils producing alternative answers should be encouraged to develop their point of view. **Worksheet 1.6a** supports this task.

Blue task: The letters on pages 43-44 provide pupils with the material to develop an empathetic piece. The task seeks to focus the pupil on the wider impact of the disturbances; once the mob was angered it targeted other unassociated symbols of authority like Newgate Prison. Asking pupils to refer to the examples thrown up by the starter should help them to recognise issues around the changing nature of demonstrations when they become riots.

Orange task: The final task draws together facts and causation in order to reach a conclusion. Pupils are asked to relate the events and reasons together in the middle of the Venn diagram to identify specific points of tension. The speculative nature of the final question should enable pupils to identify turning points, an extension of which is to consider whether all protests have such a moment, and how governments can act before they are reached.

Plenary
Question time: Is there ever a case for people to riot? Examples can be drawn from across the world and from different periods of time. For those who struggle to think of a situation, the poll tax protest photograph can be used as a stimulus to show that this type of activity can be linked to multiple causes.

ICT opportunities
In order to develop the plenary pupils could use the Internet to identify past occurrences of protest.

History in Progress – LiveText CD 2: electronic activity

1.6 Why are the people protesting?

Worksheet 1.6a: The Gordon Riots of 1780

Work out why the Gordon Riots happened. Look at the events below, which happened before the riot. Use the clues in the text to sort these events into the correct chronological order.

The Protestant Association collected a petition of 60,000 names to present to parliament during a demonstration on 2 June 1780.

In 1778 Britain was fighting wars against France, Spain and America, and needed more soldiers. All soldiers had to make a promise to fight for the king and the Protestant Church of England. But many Catholics felt they could not do this.

The government passed laws that helped Catholics by saying Catholic soldiers did not have to promise loyalty to the Church of England.

Lord George Gordon believed that being Catholic made you a traitor to the country. His group, called 'The Protestant Association', wanted the government to get rid of new laws that helped Catholics.

The demonstration to parliament got out of hand, and people started to attack known Catholics' houses and property.

1.6 Why are the people protesting?

1.6b What was the Peterloo Massacre, 1819?

Learning objectives

- To be able to use sources to produce your own account of the Peterloo Massacre.
- To be able to understand why a historical event can be interpreted in different ways.

Historical background

The end of a long war is usually a time of hope, but the introduction of a corn law in 1815 artificially inflated the price of bread, which added to the poverty caused by high unemployment. In such conditions demonstrations were almost inevitable, and after more violent assemblies the magistrates in Manchester were taking no chances with the gathering that was to take place in St Peter's Field in 1819.

Teaching Activities and Learning Outcomes

Assessment opportunity

Critically using source evidence to produce an objective historical account.

Pupils will be able to

- develop questions that challenge the validity of a source
- recognise the importance of provenance in using sources
- select further sources to enhance a point of view.

Starter

Pupils attempt the starter task on page 46 of *History in Progress – Book 2*, which highlights the fact that each of us sees the world in a different way. Pupils' first thoughts are likely to be the most strongly held beliefs. Therefore, restricting the time they have available to do this will be instrumental in achieving this.

Development

Green task: In the five questions pupils are allowed to ask the artist, some may be directed to interrogate the artist himself rather than the events in the picture, drawing out facts as to the provenance of the image. An alternative, more structured method, would be to use a 5W exercise. A simple debrief from this task might ask pupils whether they could be sure of what happened on that day from this one piece of evidence, and why.

Blue task: Sources **b–d** on page 48 are quite long, so asking pupils to explain how one of the sources adds to their knowledge would be appropriate for some of them, before asking them to consider the provenance. The newspaper report can be completed from different points of view. Ways to present this task might include a simple interview with one of the eyewitnesses to a more complex answer involving all the source material.

Orange task: Ranking **sources a–d** in order of importance should raise issues not just of provenance but on the weight that different people put on them; the Commander of the Yeomanry is more likely to be believed by those whose duty it is to uphold the law.

Plenary

Odd one out: As a quick closing exercise pupils could study three of the sources again and select the odd one out. Picking the two picture sources (**a** and **e**) and one written one will generate many differences that can be explored as time allows.

ICT opportunities

History in Progress – LiveText CD 2: electronic activity

1.6 Why are the people protesting?

1.6c Taking it further!: The Cato Street Conspiracy

Learning objectives
- Learn how the government dealt with protesters that it considered a threat
- Decide if the government's actions were justified.

Historical background
In the years following the end of the Napoleonic wars in 1815 bread prices soared, largely because of the corn laws which kept prices artificially high for the benefit of wealthy farmers, many of whom were politicians. Soldiers returned from France with revolutionary ideas to a country where jobs were scarce and poverty rife. Radical ideas quickly spread and the government, afraid of a revolution, introduced laws to control gatherings and put down protests. Activities of extremists like Arthur Thistlewood were closely tracked and the government used spies to provide them with the information they needed.

Teaching Activities and Learning Outcomes

Homework

What examples of conspiracies can pupils come up with from this and other countries?

Pupils will be able to

- make suggestions and share ideas as to the purpose of the conspiracy
- explain the actions of a government spy
- explain why the government used the methods it did to deal with protest.

Starter

Pupils work in pairs to create an ideas map listing legal ways in which people could protest. Then they rank them in order of how effective they think they would be. You could also ask pupils to consider whether violent protest is ever justified, and where they might place that on a scale of effectiveness.

Development

Task 1: Pupils could write down key words that they believe summarise the main points of each frame, before sharing these with a partner. The second part might bring up a range of answers. Class discussion as to the plotters' real purpose may be beneficial.

Task 2: Pupils think about the plot from the point of view of the spy. Some might need support to look beyond the 'he was told to' level. Discussion as to why someone might be recruited to this role might prove profitable in the creation of the diary. The concept of an 'agent provocateur' should be introduced to ensure that the stereotypical view of a spy does not prevail.

The government acted in a legally dubious manner in dealing with Thistlewood and his friends, and the second part of the task challenges the idea of 'a means to an end'. Use the outcomes of the Gordon Riot and Peterloo Massacre to review what the government could do to protesters. Encourage pairs to come up with difficult questions for both the minister and the family member to tease out issues surrounding the methods employed to resolve the plot. An alternative is a 'hot seat' activity: pupils put questions to a minister and the family member. The 'hot seat' role might be played by teacher or pupils.

Plenary

Who was right!: Vote on whether the government was right or wrong to deal with the conspirators in the way they did. Then take a second vote: if the government acted illegally by 'trapping' the men into plotting against them, do pupils think they were right or wrong?

ICT opportunities

History in Progress – LiveText CD 2: electronic activity

1.7 Who wanted the vote?

1.7a Why did people become Chartists?

Learning objectives
- To discover why people supported the Chartist movement.
- To establish a link between causes.

Historical background
At the start of the nineteenth century many people in Britain were unemployed and dependent on government aid. People wanted change but only parliament could make change. Unfortunately many middle and almost all working class men did not have the right to vote. There were slight improvements in 1832 when the Reform Bill was passed. This gave a section of the middle class the right to vote but the majority of working class men were still largely ignored. In 1838 a group of working class men gathered in Birmingham and drew up a list of six demands. This set of demands was called the 'People's Charter'. People supporting this charter were called Chartists. Their aim was to get all men the vote.

Teaching Activities and Learning Outcomes

Assessment opportunity
Making links between reasons why people chose to support Chartism and what they wanted.

Pupils will be able to
- create a spider diagram to show why people might have become Chartists
- write a charter from the point of view of a Chartist leader
- work in pairs to put together a presentation on the aims of the Chartists.

Starter
Pupils look at **source a** on page 52 of *History in Progress – Book 2*. In pairs, they describe in detail what they can see in this satirical cartoon. What type of people are voting? How is the voting taking place? What type of person is the MP? Encourage pupils to think about what is wrong with the voting process that is shown in this cartoon.

Development
Green task: Pupils should work individually to complete the spider diagram on **Worksheet 1.7a**. Those who complete this task early could be asked to rank complaints in the order of seriousness.

Blue task: Working individually pupils imagine they are Chartist leader William Lovett. Using all of the complaints explained through the lesson pupils must draw up a Charter containing six points. Make sure they are able to explain why each point is important to the Chartist cause.

Orange task: In pairs, pupils imagine they are Chartists. One pupil will explain what the Chartists wanted and the other will explain what they think will be a result of a successful Charter. They should then prepare a presentation to deliver to the rest of the class. Pupils should discuss the different sections of the speech before they deliver it to the class.

Plenary
Pupils can read their speeches to each other. Ask for positive feedback on the speeches – one thing each pupil did well and one thing each pupil could improve.

Cross-curricular links
Citizenship: Exploring how politics can make a difference to people's lives.

ICT opportunities
History in Progress – LiveText CD 2: electronic activity

1.7 Who wanted the vote?

Worksheet 1.7a Why did people become Chartists?

- Read through each of the Chartist complaints on pages 52-53 of *History in Progress – Book 2*. Use these to complete the spider diagram below explaining each of the complaints in your own words.
- Once you have done this, read through the complaints again and rank them in order of seriousness with 1 being the most serious and 6 being the least serious.

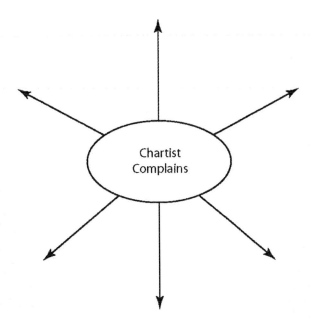

Chartist Complains

1.7 Who wanted the vote?

1.7b Chartism: the ups and downs

Learning objectives
- To find out about the rise and fall of Chartism.
- To put information in order and explain the diversity of Chartism.

Historical background
The Chartist movement was split into two main groups. The Moral Force Chartists (led by William Lovett) believed in peaceful campaigns, while the Physical Force Chartists (led by Feargus O'Connor) believed in using violence to achieve the vote. It was the failure of the different Chartist groups that contributed to Chartism's failure as a political campaign movement.

Teaching Activities and Learning Outcomes

Homework

Chartists were not the only people to campaign for the right to vote in Britain and they were not the only political group accused of using violence to protest. Pupils should research one of the following two political and protest groups for homework: the Anti-Corn Law League or the Luddites.

Pupils will be able to

- put key events of the Chartist campaign in the correct chronological order
- sort the events in peaceful or violent
- write a 250-word summary of the Chartists' aims and how they tried to achieve these.

Starter

Identify a key issue that pupils feel strongly about in school, e.g. the length of their ties, whether or not they should wear uniform. Ask pupils to suggest different ways they could campaign for/against this issue. Write these ideas on the board. Then ask pupils to identify which methods are peaceful and which are violent. Compare their ideas with ones used today by political activists, e.g. songs, wristbands, TV campaigns, dressing up and chaining themselves to political buildings.

Development

Green task: Pupils complete a timeline of Chartist activity using the graph on **Worksheet 1.7b** and decide on the success of each event. As a whole class you could read through some of the events first and decide which were a success and why, and which were a failure and why.

Blue task: Pupils examine Chartists' methods and add these to their graph. They should use the graph on **Worksheet 1.7b** to draw conclusions about why Chartism might have failed, e.g. pupils could think about the use of violent and peaceful tactics and the impact these had on the campaign.

Orange task: Write a summary of 250 words about the aims of the Chartist movement and the different types of tactics they used to attempt to achieve them. Encourage pupils to include detail in their summaries, but remind them of the word limit, which might prove a challenge for some pupils to stick to!

Plenary

Class vote: Are violent or peaceful campaign methods better for helping people to achieve their aims? Why? Link back to the fact that Chartism failed and ask them to explain why they think it failed.

Cross-curricular links

Citizenship: Linking historical campaign methods with tactics used today by political activists.

ICT opportunities

History in Progress – LiveText CD 2: electronic activity

1.7 Who wanted the vote?

Worksheet 1.7b Chartism: the ups and downs

1 Read through the events on page 55 of *History in Progress – Book 2*. Put each event in date order along the timeline on the graph below.

2 Decide whether each event was a success or failure for the Chartists. Give each event a score from -5 to +5 as follows:

3 to 5: brilliant success for the Chartists
1 to 2: positive development for the Chartists
0: neither side wins
-1 to -2: a defeat for the Chartists
-3 to -5: a disastrous defeat for the Chartists

Once you have scored each event, plot the score onto the graph.

3 Now make a note on the graph of whether you think each event used peaceful or violent tactics. What conclusions can you draw about why Chartism failed from this graph?

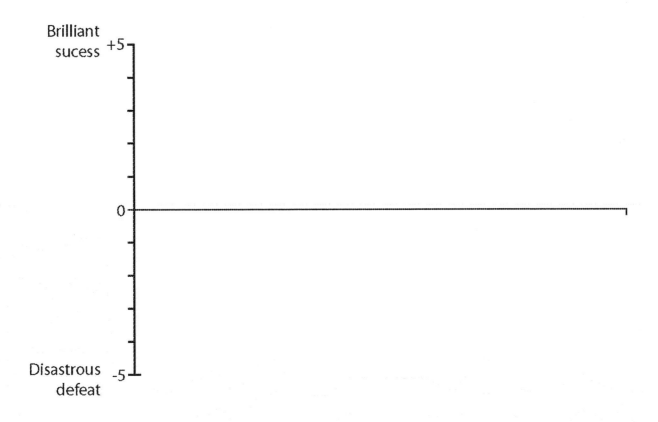

1.7 Who wanted the vote?

1.7c Taking it further!: Who was Lydia Becker?

Learning objectives
- To find out more about the status of women in the nineteenth century.
- To use sources as evidence to explain why women believed they should have the vote.

Historical background
During the nineteenth century it was not just men who wanted the vote. Women also believed in the Chartist cause and after Chartism ended they still kept pushing for reform. One such woman was Lydia Becker, who worked with other women in 1886 to set up the Manchester Women's Suffrage Committee to campaign for women to have the right to vote.

Teaching Activities and Learning Outcomes

Assessment opportunity

Working with source material, making inferences and supporting own points of view about the importance of Lydia Becker with evidence from the sources.

Pupils will be able to

- form an opinion about Lydia Becker and justify this
- share their opinion with a partner, and identify reasons for similarities and differences between their points of view.

Starter

Write the following statements on the board for when the pupils arrive. This should spark a starter debate as to whether the statements are accurate or not.

- *Women are not as intelligent as men.*
- *Criminals, lunatics and drunks should be able to vote, and women should not be allowed to vote.*
- *Women are the property of their husbands and should do as they are told.*

Use the discussion generated here to link into why women were not allowed to vote in the nineteenth century.

Development

- **Tasks 1–3:** These require pupils to apply comprehension and inference skills to **sources a–e** on pages 56-57 of *History in Progress – Book 2*. Once they have identified Becker's main ideas and methods, they should use this information to infer what sort of a person she was. These tasks offer a good opportunity for peer-assessment to take place. Pupils compare their ideas about Becker with a partner to see if they share the same opinions. Ask pupils to think carefully about why there might be differences in their opinions. What evidence from the sources have they used to form their views?

Plenary

Pupils each explain one reason why they think Lydia Becker was important in the ongoing campaign for women in Great Britain to achieve the vote.

Cross-curricular links

Citizenship: Establishing different reasons why universal suffrage was important for everybody in Great Britain.

ICT opportunities

History in Progress – LiveText CD 2: electronic activity

Unit 1 Ruling

1.8 Making connections: Who held power between 1603 and 1901?

Learning objectives
- To understand who held most power: the monarch, parliament, men or women.
- To show an understanding of change over time.

Historical background
In 1603 power resided overwhelmingly with the monarch but during the following decades parliament began to challenge the power of the king, demanding greater powers for itself, as the representative of the people. However, it was only by the reign of Victoria that parliament's authority was consistently greater than that of the crown, which had become a figurehead with important potential but latent powers, such as the right to veto parliamentary legislation. It should also be remembered that the power of ordinary people increased only slowly during the nineteenth century as the Reform Acts gradually expanded the franchise, but women remained without the vote until 1918!

Teaching Activities and Learning Outcomes

Assessment opportunity
Change over time.

Pupils will be able to
- chart the fluctuations in the amount of power held by the monarch, parliament, men and women
- draw conclusions about who held the most power, and how this varied over time.

Starter
Gimme 5: Pupils suggest five ways in which who holds power has changed from 1603 to 1901.

Development
- **Green task:** Pupils select key events and use these to chart the relative power of the monarchy, parliament, men and women on a graph. A worksheet template (**Worksheet 1.8**) is provided. Remind pupils that there is no right answer to the exact shape of their graph and suggest they mark in coloured pencil so they can make adjustments more easily.
- **Blue task:** Pupils compare their graphs (perhaps agreeing on a whole-class graph on the board). They could then discuss the overall changes: that parliament rather than the monarchy was more powerful by the end of the period in contrast to the start of the graph; that times of dramatic change, e.g. during the Civil War, did not bring about lasting change immediately (since the monarch was returned with full powers in 1660); but that it did increase the confidence of parliament, which encouraged it to act more strongly later (when it invited William of Orange to be King instead of James II).
- **Orange task:** Pupils discuss in pairs whether they agree with the statements; remind them to back up their verdict using evidence they have come across during the unit.

Plenary
Time for reflection: Ask pupils who holds the most power today and if they think this is right. Discuss who votes for parliament today and how this is different from the period they have just studied.

Cross-curricular links
Citizenship: Key features of parliamentary democracy and government.

ICT opportunities
History in Progress – LiveText CD 2: electronic activity

Unit 1 Ruling

Worksheet 1.8 Who held power between 1603 and 1901?

1 Choose five or six events that you have studied and that you think changed who held the power in Britain. Add these to the timeline at the bottom of your graph.

2 Draw onto the graph a cross for each event to show how much power the monarch had. Now join up these crosses.

3 Now draw crosses onto your graph to show the power of parliament at each event and use another colour to join these up. Take another colour pencil and do the same for middle and working class men, and then a fourth colour for middle and working class women.

4 When you have completed your graph, compare your lines with a partner. Discuss in pairs what you notice about your lines and what this tells you about the how the power shifted between 1603 and 1901.

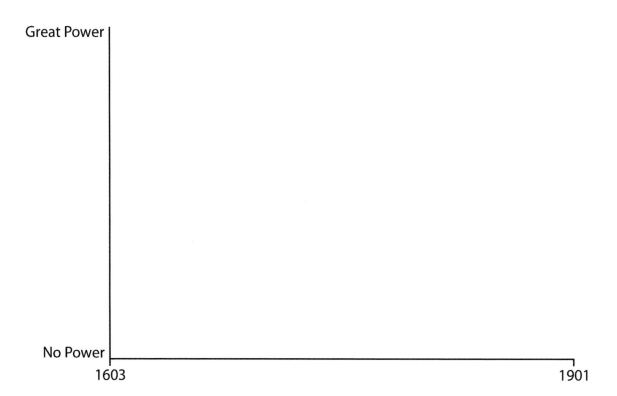

Unit 1 Ruling

Assessment Unit 1

1.9 Assessment task 1: Charles I: martyr or tyrant? Why has Charles I been remembered in different ways?

Pupils will be able to

- evaluate the reasons why different interpretations exist.

What the task is about

- The focus of this assessment task is interpretation.
- Pupils should read through **sources a-c** on page 60 of *History in Progress – Book 2*. They may require help understanding source b. If so point out the way Charles is depicted as religious, humble and Christ-like (the crown of thorns) and how the light of heaven seems to be shining on him, suggesting he is king by divine right, implying that to execute him was not just treason but a sin, too.
- The questions become more challenging; outline guidance on how best to structure the answers is given on page 61.
- It is intended that pupils answer the questions on their own, using **Worksheet 1.9a** as a guide if necessary. However, it is possible for the questions to be set as part of a group-work exercise with responses to **task 3** to be fed back as part of a whole-class discussion.
- Pupils might wish to use the Internet to research alternative interpretations of Charles.
- Pupils move up the levels from Level 4 to 6 with successful completion of all questions. The assessment task is designed so that there is differentiation by task. A mark scheme is provided on **Worksheet 1.9b**.
- This task can be undertaken either after completion of **Enquiry 1.1** or at the end of the unit.

Assessment task 2: Was revolution the road to freedom? How much changed as a result of the revolutions in England, America and France?

Pupils will be able to

- compare the significance of the revolutions in England, America and France in bringing freedom and equality to the people.

What the task is about

- The focus of this assessment task is comparing the significance of the revolutions in leading to liberty and equality for the people of each country.
- The first step is for pupils to fill in the table. Pupils can use the **Worksheet 1.10a(i)** to complete this part of the task. This can be done by referring to earlier work studied as part of this unit.
- **Task 2** could be a discussion task with pupils working in pairs to come up with a verdict on each statement, which could then be fed back through class discussion for further comparison debate. Pupils should be reminded of the need to justify their verdict with evidence from the completed table.
- **Task 3** provides the opportunity to assess a piece of extended writing. It is intended that the pupils answer the question independently. Encourage pupils to plan their answer – **Worksheet 1.10a(ii)** provides a suggested outline for pupils to follow.
- Pupils move up the levels from Level 4 to 6 with successful completion of all questions. The assessment task is designed so that there is differentiation by task. A mark scheme is provided on **Worksheet 1.10b**.
- This exercise can be undertaken either after the completion of **Enquiry 1.5** or at the end of the unit.

ICT opportunities

History in Progress – LiveText CD 2: electronic activities

Unit 1 Assessment 1

Worksheet 1.9a

Charles I: martyr or tyrant? Why has Charles I been remembered in different ways?

1 Look at **sources a–c** on page 60 of *History in Progress – Book* 2 and complete the following table to show what impression of Charles I each source gives you.

Source a	Source b	Source c

2 Take a coloured pen or pencil and highlight any differences you can see between the impression given of Charles I in **sources b** and **c**.

3 Suggest at least two reasons why **sources a, b** and **c** give different impressions of Charles I?

_____

_____

_____

4 Give two reasons why **sources b** and **c** differ in their interpretations of Charles I.

_____

_____

_____

Unit 1 Assessment 1

Worksheet 1.9b

Charles I: martyr or tyrant? Why has Charles I been remembered in different ways?

How did you do?

Level 4: I was able to ...

identify and describe different ways in which the past has been interpreted.	
use the right sort of information to answer the question.	
produce structured work.	

Level 5: I was able to ...

suggest some reasons for different interpretations of the past.	
select and use information from the sources as examples.	
produce work which is carefully structured.	

Level 6: I was able to ...

explain how and why different interpretations of the past have arisen or been constructed.	
select and use relevant information from the sources as examples.	
produce work which is carefully and clearly structured.	

Things I did well: _____

I need to learn more about: _____

One thing I need to improve is: _____

I will do this by: _____

Teacher comment: _____

Pupil comment: _____

Unit 1 Assessment 2

Worksheet 1.10a(i)

Was revolution the road to freedom? How much changed as a result of the revolutions in England, America and France?

For each of the revolutions you have studied in this unit complete a column in the table below. To help you, use what you have learned about each revolution in *History in Progress – Book 2*, Unit 1 'Ruling'.

	England	America	France
1 Who held most power before the revolution?			
2 Who/what held most power after the revolution?			
3 Was the revolution peaceful or violent?			
4 After the revolution could a wealthy man who owned his own property vote?			
5 Could a poor man vote?			
6 Could a woman vote?			
7 Were any groups still discriminated against after the revolution?			
8 Were all religions respected equally after the revolution?			
9 Did people have more rights and freedoms after the revolution?			

Unit 1 Assessment 2

Worksheet 1.10a(ii)

Was revolution the road to freedom? How much changed as a result of the revolutions in England, America and France?

Plan your answer to this question. Use the suggestions below to help you make notes of what you want to include in each paragraph. You might choose to look at more than one revolution, in which case you will need to expand this plan.

Paragraph 1: Explain how people in Britain/America/France felt that they were ruled unfairly before the revolutions because … _____

_____

_____

_____

Paragraph 2: Explain how after the revolutions the governments were designed to be fairer, e.g. … _____

_____

_____

_____

Paragraph 3: Explain how the new governments aimed to bring more freedom and better rights for the people, e.g. … _____

_____

_____

_____

Paragraph 4: Explain how not everyone benefited from the change in governments, e.g. …

_____

_____

_____

_____

Paragraph 5: Overall, the change in government was most successful in … (choose a country) because

_____

_____

_____

_____

Unit 1 Assessment 2

Worksheet 1.10b

Was revolution the road to freedom? How much changed as a result of the revolutions in England, America and France?

How did you do?

Level 4: I was able to …

describe some different interpretations of the past	
identify and use some information from the sources as examples to back up your points	
produce work which showed some structure	

Level 5: I was able to …

describe some of the changes brought about by the revolutions.	
select and use information as examples.	
produce work which is carefully structured.	
describe my judgement about which revolution was most successful.	

Level 6: I was able to …

explain the extent of change brought about by each revolution.	
select and use relevant information as examples.	
produce work which is carefully and clearly structured.	
attempt to explain my judgment about which revolution was most successful.	

Things I did well: _____

I need to learn more about: _____

One thing I need to improve is: _____

I will do this by: _____

Teacher comment: _____

Pupil comment: _____

2.1 What frightened people in the seventeenth century?

2.1a Deadly diseases

Learning objectives
- To find out how members of the Verney family lived and died.
- To weigh up how dangerous a threat disease was to people in the seventeenth century.

Historical background
Disease and death were major concerns for anyone living in the seventeenth century. The greatest killer came in 1665 with the return of the plague which most affected London. However, more consistent killers were childhood diseases and, for women, childbirth. Medicine in the seventeenth century tended to be based on superstition, due to the lack of scientific understanding about the causes of disease.

Teaching Activities and Learning Outcomes

Homework

Research some of the methods used for prevention and cure of the plague in the seventeenth century.

Pupils will be able to

- select information from a family tree about causes and frequency of death in the seventeenth century
- draw conclusions from sources about the causes of death and health care in the seventeenth century
- write a guide to healthcare and dangers in the seventeenth century, using evidence to support ideas.

Starter

Pupils use the family tree on page 66 of *History in Progress – Book 2* and note what surprises them or is different to what they would expect in a modern family tree, e.g. the relatively large number of children in the family, the number of children who died in infancy, deaths from childbirth, the age people died.

Development

Green task: Pupils record precise information selected from the family tree. They might mention as surprising: the number of infant deaths (due to lack of scientific knowledge about how to prevent childhood diseases through, e.g. inoculations); the wide disparity in ages (some clearly lived until they were very old; that in a wealthy family like the Verney's, once you had grown beyond childhood you stood a good chance of living a long time.

Blue task: Pupils select information from the sources to explain the problems with healthcare in the seventeenth century. They should note the difficulty of developing effective cures since the causes of disease were unknown. As a result people relied on more superstitious remedies. The Verney's were less affected by the plague than others because they, like many wealthy people left London for the duration of the plague. For this reason, the 1665 outbreak was known as the 'poor man's plague'.

Orange task: Pupils use the knowledge they have gained to produce a good health guide for the seventeenth century. Pupils should be encouraged to structure their guide/poster/pamphlet with care, and to show the causes, and suggested cures.

Plenary

Pupils work in pairs to suggest two differences between medicine in the seventeenth century and medicine today, e.g. better understanding of the causes of disease, more preventative medicine.

Cross-curricular links

Science: The development of healthcare.

ICT opportunities

History in Progress - LiveText CD 2: electronic activity

2.1 What frightened people in the seventeenth century?

2.1b Why people were accused of witchcraft

Learning objectives
- To investigate what happened during the witch hunts in Essex and Suffolk in the1640s.
- To understand the causes of the witch hunts.

Historical background
A witch hunt centred on Essex and Suffolk in the 1640s during which about 300 people, mainly elderly women, were denounced and interrogated as witches. Although a belief in the power of the devil and in witches had existed for hundreds of years, there had never been a witch hunt on such a large scale in England. It is likely that the witch craze occurred due to the increased hardships of people during the Civil War who sought scapegoats and explanations for their misfortune by blaming these elderly women.

Teaching Activities and Learning Outcomes

Assessment opportunity
Causal understanding.

Pupils will be able to
- identify common causes in accusations of witch craft from different case studies
- explain the main causes of the witch hunts in the 1640s
- write a persuasive piece criticising the witch craft denunciations as unfounded.

Starter
Pupils generate images they think of when witches are mentioned. They will probably suggest old women, black cats, disfigurement, spells, misfortunes. Pupils will be able to see how far people denounced as witches in the seventeenth century reflected these preconceptions.

Development
Green task: Pupils prepare a list of questions they would ask the Witchfinder General to help them defend their chosen suspect at a witchcraft trial. Their questions should be based on the information provided on pages 68-69 of *History in Progress – Book 2*.

Blue task: Pupils now examine the evidence on page 69, which the defence lawyer would use in the case for the suspected witch. Pupils should note that the accusations of witchcraft came from communities who were suffering poverty and who sought someone to blame for their problems (especially health problems; because they had no scientific explanation for disease, superstition and spells were often blamed). Old women, who were unpopular, were often scapegoats since people disliked them and felt they often relied on handouts for survival which took food away from others.

Orange task: Pupils write a persuasive piece for the trial of one of the suspects, arguing that she is innocent, the denunciations are unfair and that Margaret has been made the scapegoat for the town's problems. These pieces could be read out at a reconstructed trial.

Plenary
Back to the start: This provides the opportunity to summarise the dangers in the seventeenth century considered in the previous two lessons. This could form the basis of a discussion and vote as to the most and least dangerous features of life.

ICT opportunities
History in Progress - LiveText CD 2: electronic activity

2.1 What frightened people in the seventeenth century?

2.1c Taking it further!: Great Fire of London: accident or arson?

Learning objectives
- To understand the causes of the Great Fire of London in 1666.
- To evaluate different interpretations of what caused the fire.

Historical background
The Great Fire of London began in 1666 and destroyed huge areas of the city. After the fire a monument (simply called Monument) was erected in London with a plaque laying the blame for the fire on Robert Hubert, a Frenchman who, it was believed, was part of a Catholic conspiracy. He was hanged for the crime. However, the verdict was probably the result of popular anti-Catholic hysteria at the time. The fire was more likely started by accident in a bakery at the end of a long hot summer when the wooden buildings were dried out and the flames were fanned by a strong easterly wind. One positive result was that by destroying everything, the fire eradicated the plague which had been having a devastating effect.

Teaching Activities and Learning Outcomes

Assessment opportunity

Using evidence to support different causal interpretations.

Pupils will be able to

- select evidence from sources to support explanations about what caused the fire
- evaluate the reliability of sources to reach a conclusion about the causes of the fire.

Starter

If pupils have heard of the Great Fire ask them to share what they know with a partner. Alternatively, a description or image of Monument in London, which commemorates the fire, could be used. Pupils could be told of the inscription blaming the Frenchman, Hubert, for starting the fire. Encourage them to think about whether this was likely to be true, or propaganda.

Development

This task could be completed in a variety of ways. Statement cards are provided on **Worksheet 2.1c** to make sorting the evidence easier.
- Pupils fill out a table with reasons that support and undermine the statement.
- Alternatively, divide the class into groups to collect evidence either for or against the accusation. This could precede a debate or a trial of Hubert on the charge of starting the fire. Pupils could prepare questions to cross examine Hubert.
- Encourage pupils to consider the reliability of the sources. They might highlight that Hubert's evidence is dubious, he seems of unsound mind, and there was much popular anti-French and anti-Catholic sentiment in England at the time which might have led to his conviction (especially given memories of the Gunpowder Plot of 1605). The evidence of Thomas Farriner, the baker, is similarly dubious, given that he would want to emphasise his innocence.

Plenary

If a trial has been held, then a vote about the guilt of Hubert could close the trial. Alternatively, pupils could vote to show their overall view about the truth of the claim that the fire was started by foreign spies. Pupils are likely to conclude that the fire was not started by foreign spies, which may prompt a discussion about why this was not the verdict in the seventeenth century.

ICT opportunities

History in Progress - LiveText CD 2: electronic activity

2.1 What frightened people in the seventeenth century?

Worksheet 2.1c Great Fire of London: accident or arson?

> ### *The fire was caused deliberately by foreign spies.*

Sort the evidence below to back up your opinion of this statement. Give examples to justify your view and explain why you think the opposite view is incorrect.

A

Thomas Farriner owned the bakery in Pudding Lane. He said that 'he had after 12 o'clock that night gone through every room and found no fire but one in the chimney, where the room was paved with bricks, this fire he diligently raked to embers'. He was sure the fire was started later on purpose.

B

The bakery had a large oven, above which was stored chopped wood ready for the next day. All the houses were tightly packed together and were made of wood that was particularly dry from months of drought.

C

On the night of 2 September there was a strong easterly wind. This may have blown a spark from the fire onto the chopped wood. The gale blew for four days, spreading the fire. Neighbours accused Thomas Farriner of returning home drunk.

D

In a cellar further down Pudding Lane twelve barrels of tar were stored which when heated by the fire exploded like a bomb.

E

Men rushed to the church to collect buckets, but they found these either stolen or damaged. Basic fire engines arrived but were ineffective because at low tide there was not enough water in the pipes under the ground to operate the water jets. Firehooks (which were used to pull down buildings and stop fire by denying it the fuel to burn) were found, but the Lord Mayor of London told people not to use them because he did not want to pay compensation for the damage. The fire was halted four days later, partly because houses were pulled down.

F

Rumours spread that fireballs were being thrown by foreigners and Catholics (England at the time was a mainly Protestant country) because some houses close to, but not directly next to, the flames caught fire. One witness said he saw 'a Frenchman in the act of firing a house in Shoe Lane'. At the time England was at war with France and Holland. England also feared attacks from Catholics.

G

The Frenchman Robert Hubert was hanged in October 1666 for starting the fire. Hubert confessed that he came ashore in London on 2 September, went to the baker's house, placed a fireball on the end of a long pole and put it through a window. Hubert made many confessions, all were slightly different and he was most probably tortured.

H

Lawrence Petersen, a ship's captain, said that Robert Hubert had been a passenger on his ship. He remembered arriving in London and keeping Hubert in his cabin until 4 September 1666, when he escaped. Petersen said that Hubert had a weak mind, was mad, spoke no real English, and had a paralysed right leg and arm.

2.2 What was life like for immigrants in Britain?

2.2a Huguenot and Jewish immigrants

Learning objectives
- To discover the different skills that Jewish and Huguenot immigrants brought to England.
- To explore the impact of immigration on London's economy, society and industry.

Historical background
During the eighteenth and nineteenth centuries Jewish and Huguenot immigrants made their home in the East End of London. They developed an enriching and multicultural society in Spitalfields and on Brick Lane. The immigrants brought a wealth of new skills and industry to Great Britain such as kosher butchers, the silk industry, and silversmith, banking and watchmaking skills.

Teaching Activities and Learning Outcomes

Assessment opportunity

Making links between the different reasons why people chose to support Chartism.

Pupils will be able to

- list five positive impacts immigrants had on London
- complete a chart to help them decide which community had the greatest impact
- write a letter from an immigrant's point of view explaining whether or not their family should emigrate.

Starter

Pupils look at **source a** on page 72 of *History in Progress – Book 2*, showing the Jamme Masjid Mosque in East London. Ask them to read the information about how this building has changed religion over the last 250 years. They can then discuss in pairs or small groups what this suggests about the changing cultures in the East End of London.

Development

Green task: Pupils select five positive impacts that immigrants had on London society. They should be prepared to explain their selection and could compare their five choices with a partner before moving on to discuss any possible negative impacts.

Blue task: Pupils re-examine all of the evidence and make a decision regarding how immigrant groups contributed to London life. **Worksheet 2.2a** supports this task. They should summarise their ideas in a paragraph explaining which immigrant group made the biggest contribution to London society. Encourage pupils to use facts from their table to support their ideas.

Orange task: Pupils now use all the information from this lesson to write a letter to a member of their family living abroad encouraging them to travel to London for work. They should draw together in this letter all the ideas from the lesson. An idea for its structure is provided on page 73 of *History in Progress – Book 2*. Pupils should also be reminded about the conventions of letter writing – how to start the letter and end it.

Plenary

Pupils work in pairs to identify what they think is the most important skill that immigrants contributed to society in the eighteenth century. They should share their idea with the class and explain their choice.

Cross-curricular links

Religious Education: Evaluating the impact of different religious groups on London.

ICT opportunities

History in Progress - LiveText CD 2: electronic activity

2.2 What was life like for immigrants in Britain?

Worksheet 2.2a: Huguenot and Jewish immigrants

Complete the table below identifying the different contributions that Jewish and Huguenot immigrants made to London society in the eighteenth and nineteenth centuries.

Jewish contributions to London society	Huguenot contributions to London society

2.2 What was life like for immigrants in Britain?

2.2b Free black communities in eighteenth- and nineteenth-century Britain

Learning objectives
- To understand the diversity of black people's lives in eighteenth- and nineteenth-century Britain.
- To use pictures as historical evidence.

Historical background
Many people believe that the only black communities in eighteenth-century Britain were slaves. However, by the late eighteenth century there was actually a large free black community in London. Slave traders who had returned from America after the British lost the War of Independence brought slaves with them as free servants for their new households. Some freed slaves also found employment in the British and Merchant navies, and they were often seen around the Port of London. Black soldiers who had fought with the British army as Loyalists during the American War of Independence in return for their freedom emigrated to London when Britain lost the war.

Teaching Activities and Learning Outcomes

Assessment opportunity

Evaluating pictures as evidence to form part of an historical enquiry.

Pupils will be able to

- describe three relevant points from each source
- use their ideas to explain what the sources tell them about black people in Britain
- draw conclusions about the attitudes towards black people of each artist.

Starter

Ask pupils to describe what type of jobs they think a freed black slave would be qualified to do in London during the eighteenth century. Then lead a class discussion towards whether pupils feel these new jobs actively improved the lives of the free black community in London.

Development

Green task: Pupils describe three points from each source (b–d; pages 74-75 of *History in Progress – Book 2*) about the black community in Britain in the eighteenth and nineteenth centuries. Encourage pupils to focus on what the people are doing in these pictures, where they appear to be and what the people around them are doing.

Blue task: Pupils develop further information from task 1. Encourage them to identify how the sources provide information about work, leisure and lifestyle at the time; more able pupils could be asked to suggest other possible groupings.

Orange task: This task utilises all the work that pupils have previously completed during this lesson. Pupils will need to re-examine the picture sources to make a decision about how artists mainly felt about black people in the eighteenth and nineteenth centuries. Pupils will need to explain their overall decision using concise and clear language.

Plenary

Three in a row: At least three pupils in the class must get three questions right in a row before they can pack away. If an answer is wrong or someone shouts out, the questioning should start again.

ICT opportunities

History in Progress - LiveText CD 2: electronic activity

2.2 What was life like for immigrants in Britain?

2.2c Taking it further!: Mary Seacole and the Crimean War

Learning objectives

- To develop an understanding of the role played by Mary Seacole during the Crimean War.
- To use contemporary sources to evaluate the importance of an individual during a period of difficulty.

Historical background

During the 1850s, Britain became involved in a war against Russia called the Crimean War. One of the worst aspects of this war was the horrendous hospital conditions that wounded soldiers faced in British field hospitals and the outbreaks of cholera that accompanied these conditions. For many years historians have linked the Crimean War with Florence Nightingale's efforts to improve hospital cleanliness and nursing. They did not write about other important members of the British Empire who travelled to the Crimea to help soldiers. One such person was Mary Seacole.

Teaching Activities and Learning Outcomes

Homework

There is great scope here for an extended lesson on Mary Seacole. Pupils will be asked in the lesson to produce a newspaper report. A good homework task would be for pupils to take their investigation of Seacole further. You could ask them to produce one of the following to present to the rest of the class:

- a PowerPoint presentation about the life of Mary Seacole
- a written report on the life of Mary Seacole
- an oral presentation to be delivered to the rest of the class.

Pupils will be able to

- write a newspaper report about Mary Seacole in no more than 300 words.

Starter

Ask pupils to look **source a**, an image of Mary Seacole, on page 76 of *History in Progress – Book 2*. They should work in pairs to create a series of questions they might ask the person in the picture to find out information about why they were important in British history.

Development

Pupils imagine it is 1857 and they are a reporter for *The Times* newspaper. When giving pupils their instructions you can assume the role of newspaper editor and ask them to interview a recent arrival in London called Mary Seacole. Provide pupils with information from the pupil book and inform them that she played an important role in helping British soldiers who were injured during the Crimean War. Explain that, as space in the newspaper is limited, their articles must not exceed 300 words. This is a good opportunity for pupils to prepare a succinct and carefully edited piece of writing.

Plenary

Each pupil in the class should provide one new fact that they have learned in the lesson without repeating another person's answer.

Cross-curricular links

Media: Students will use their historical information to help them produce a newspaper media report.

ICT opportunities

History in Progress - LiveText CD 2: electronic activity

2.3 Was the Qing Dynasty educated, cultured and equal?

2.3a Qing Dynasty homes

Learning objectives
- To investigate Yin Yu Tang, a late Qing Dynasty merchant's home.
- To evaluate the role of museums in the preservation and conservation of sites.

Historical background
Chinese architecture is full of symbolism from its interaction with the landscape and materials used for construction, to decorative features inside and outside of the house. Little was placed for aesthetic beauty alone. Chinese architecture reveals the importance of family as houses were built to take several generations of family at one time. Yin Yu Tang is an original merchant house from the Qing Dynasty. It has been relocated to a museum in the USA. It has its own website and presents a fascinating opportunity to study architecture from the period and the importance of museum preservation work.

Teaching Activities and Learning Outcomes

Assessment opportunity

Task 3: Evaluating the importance of the preservation of historical architecture.

Pupils will be able to

- describe significant features of a Qing Dynasty period house in the form of an estate agent's advert
- describe how the house was transported to a museum site in the USA and explain why this was done
- explain the importance of preservation and what preserved historical architecture can tell us.

Starter

Pupils draw a plan of their own house. They should label all the rooms and explain why they think the house was designed in that way. They must describe what features of the house are unique and explain why a person in the future would want to preserve those features. They must then explain what could be learned about the present from the preservation of those features.

Development

- **Green task:** Pupils create an estate agent's advert for Yin Yu Tang. More able pupils will question who the target market will be. To increase difficulty, the target market could be the Peabody Essex Museum in which case pupils will have to emphasise the historical significance of each feature.
- **Blue task:** This is a high order thinking activity. Encourage pupils to refine their thinking and consider how much global awareness of Chinese culture would have been enhanced by leaving the house *in situ*. Pupils could also consider if we value what is around us every day or would it be necessary to transport it thousands of miles at an enormous cost to understand its significance. **Worksheet 2.3a** supports this task.
- **Orange task:** Having explained the comments of William Morris, pupils form opinions about the importance of preservation by explaining what can be learned from preserved historical buildings. Pupils can contextualise understanding in architectural features local to their own area.

Plenary

Pupils collectively create a thought shower of what they have learned about Chinese society from the study of Yin Yu Tang. They then decide if preservation is worth the money, the time and the effort.

ICT opportunities

Go to www.heinemann.co.uk/hotlinks for a detailed website on Qing Dynasty homes.

History in Progress - LiveText CD 2: electronic activity

Was the Qing Dynasty educated, cultured and equal?

Worksheet 2.3a Qing Dynasty homes

The cards below show all the tasks that had to be carried out to rebuild Yin Yu Tang in another place. Working in pairs, sort the tasks into those that:

- were taken to ensure the symbolism of the house was maintained
- would have been most difficult to manage
- would have been most expensive.

A spiritual ceremony was held by the remaining members of the Huang family to hand the house from their ancestors to the Museum.

Detailed drawings were made and measurements taken including the relationship of the house with the landscape while the house was still intact.

Bamboo scaffolding was placed around the house.

Each wooden and stone component was labelled including the symbolic chopsticks and coins that were found.

Fragile components such as the lattice windows were taken out first.

Roof tiles were removed one by one.

All components were packaged up in custom-made crates for shipping.

On arrival all crates were unloaded in custom-built warehouses.

Repairs were made by master craftsmen to components of the house that had been ruined over the life of the house. Expert craftsmen were brought from China to complete the symbolic carvings.

Structural engineers, preservation architects, curators and timber frame specialists began to re-erect the house.

2.3 Was the Qing Dynasty educated, cultured and equal?

2.3b The life of a Qing Dynasty woman

Learning objectives
- To investigate attitudes towards women that defined their role during the Qing Dynasty in China.
- To develop empathy of cultural and ethnic diversity within and across societies.

Historical background
During the Qing Dynasty Taiwan, Chinese Central Asia, Mongolia and Tibet were all attached to China. The population grew rapidly and by the end of the eighteenth century China had a population of at least 300 million people. By 1850 it was over 400 million. China felt it did not have to trade with the rest of the world as it had all she would ever need. She felt foreign nations were inferior and should be kept away as they would infect China with Western ways.

Teaching Activities and Learning Outcomes

Assessment opportunity

Empathising with cultural and ethnic diversity within and across societies.

Pupils will be able to

- identify features of the role of Qing Dynasty women
- appreciate differing attitudes among Qing Dynasty women at the time
- list similarities and differences of Qing and seventeenth- and eighteenth-century European women.

Starter

Using **Worksheet 2.3b** to establish prior knowledge, pupils identify what they can see, what they can infer and what else they need to know on the subject of Qing women. Use this opportunity to build pupils' questions into the objectives of the lesson. Also by asking pupils to examine the source they must use all of their senses as an introduction to the empathy task that follows in the main body of the lesson.

Development

- **Green task:** Pupils use **sources a–c** on page 80 of *History in Progress – Book 2* and extract features of the role of women.
- **Blue task:** This task highlights that when asked to empathise with the past we sometimes get it wrong. Most pupils will talk about developing fashions and how it showed a woman was high status, as she would have to be accompanied or carried everywhere. It also shows women's fear they would not find a husband, as the lotus foot was an attractive characteristic. More able pupils will deduce it was a way to deny subservience to an invading force and prevent intermarriage between Manchus and traditional Chinese.
- **Orange task:** Pupils, tentatively, have formed an opinion of the nature of Qing Dynasty Chinese based on information so far. This task asks them to explore the similarities of this tradition with European corset wearing happening at the same time, exploring similarities across cultures.

Plenary

Pupils review their work on **Worksheet 2.3a**. Using a different-coloured pen they should develop their responses using the knowledge they have gained in the lesson. Questions they still need to answer will form the basis of the starter for the next lesson or a good homework.

ICT opportunities

Research into the poetry of Wang Yun who illustrates the suppressed intellect of a Qing Dynasty woman.

History in Progress - LiveText CD 2: electronic activity

Was the Qing Dynasty educated, cultured and equal?
Worksheet 2.3b The life of a Qing Dynasty woman

What do you know about women in the Qing Dynasty?

LE LYS D'OR

2.4 Why did the American Indians move west?

2.4a Who were the Seminole?

Learning objectives
- To learn about the diverse origins of the Seminole Indians of Florida.
- To use sources to investigate the culture, and ethnic diversity of the Seminole peoples.

Historical background
While not as familiar as the stories of the Wild West, the Seminole's story is one that gives clear indications of what was to follow for American Indians. The generic name Seminole hides behind it a complex mixture of many different tribes, who each found their way to Florida in search of new lands at the turn of the eighteenth century as the Spanish empire declined.

Teaching Activities and Learning Outcomes

Assessment opportunity

Selecting relevant information about the background of the Seminole Indians; making links between diverse source materials; constructing historical narrative from selected sources

Pupils will be able to

- state the origins of the Seminole Indians
- locate information from the text to explain the background of the Seminoles
- present and contextually discuss the historical nature of the Seminole Indians.

Starter

What do you know? This exercise is best conducted working on an individual basis at first, before asking pupils to work with a partner to pick out similar phrases/key words with the images from the lesson unavailable to them. A follow-up could ask where they have drawn this information from and whether there are questions to be raised about how valid their answers might be.

Development

Green task: Sources b and **c** from pages 83-84 of *History in Progress – Book 2* can be compared to highlight features such as chronology and colonial power, and to identify why the Seminole could migrate quite easily to these lands. Pupils use key facts uncovered here as part of their fact file.

Blue task: The sources themselves are largely single-tribe based to help pupils recognise the number of differing tribes. Different colours can be used to identify specific reasons when linking – such as movement because of conflict. Once completed, the mind map can be analysed by using the device of a conversation with a Seminole Indian talking about their history.

Orange task: Worksheet 2.4a helps pupils to structure their work and extra material to provide more background. Pupils can complete this task in a number of other ways, e.g. a booklet or presentational piece. Challenge and differentiation can be added by defining the type of audience they are writing for. Sharing a list of characteristics of what a successful piece of work looks like enables peer-assessment, with judgements based on these characteristics.

Plenary

Control pad: Pupils consider what they have discovered about the Seminole by writing down the four symbols from a games controller to bring their ideas together. **Circle:** The big idea, a broad statement of what has been learnt; **Triangle:** three main points from the lesson; **Square:** four significant pieces of detail; **Cross:** one thing that they have not understood OR they would like to know more about.

ICT opportunities

History in Progress - LiveText CD 2: electronic activity

2.4 Why did the American Indians move west?

Worksheet 2.4a(i) Who were the Seminole?

Using information from this lesson and further research, list what you know about the Seminole Indians.

Who were the Seminoles?

_____

_____

Where did they come from?

_____

_____

_____

Which part of America did they settle in?

_____

_____

They looked like:

_____

_____

_____

They lived in:

_____

_____

_____

A famous Seminole chief was:

_____

He was famous because:

_____

_____

An interest fact about the Seminole Indians is:

_____

_____

They are different because:

_____

_____

2.4 Why did the American Indians move west?

Worksheet 2.4a(ii) Who were the Seminole?

Here is a list of some more information about the Seminole tribe. To use this information you will need to order it depending on how you have chosen to present your Seminole fact file. Remember to think about the audience you are aiming your fact file at.

- 1822: Roughly 5,000–6,000 Seminole lived in 34 villages, mainly in the northern half of Florida.

- 1780s: Seminoles fought with the British against the Americans to stop American raiding parties who wanted to recover runaway slaves.

- First Seminole war 1817: Fought against United States against Jackson – 300 Indian villages destroyed.

- By 1750 the tribes had built towns along the Suwannee River, linked to villages by roads and marriage between the groups.

- Black Seminoles lived in their own independent villages, elected their own leaders and could own cattle and crops and have their own weapons.

- 1823: Seminole tribe moved to a reservation in central Florida by Treaty of Moultrie Creek.

- 1812: Seminole Indians attacked white American 'patriot' armies in Florida who were in search of 'free' land.

- Black Seminole men only had one wife, whereas Red Seminoles married a first wife and could marry other wives later.

- 1821: Spain 'sells' Florida to USA.

- 1814: Battle of Horseshoe Bend – Creek Indians heavily defeated by General Andrew Jackson. The Creek Indians moved south to join with the Seminoles.

- There has never been a single 'Seminole' language. Muskogee was the language of treaties and trade agreements. Some Seminole spoke Muskogee, while others spoke Mikasuki.

2.4 Why did the American Indians move west?

2.4b Black Seminoles

Learning objectives
- To be able to understand why Black people became Seminole Indians.
- To be able to use sources to reach a conclusion.

Historical background
As the plantations of the south-eastern states of America grew, slaves were brought across from Africa to meet the demand for labour. Many slaves took tremendous risks to regain their freedom by escaping to Florida, where the Spanish welcomed them as free men, and the Seminole tribes gave them an identity. As increasing numbers of slaves escaped into Florida, black Seminole communities were established and became an important part of the Seminole nation.

Teaching Activities and Learning Outcomes

Assessment opportunity
Selecting and deploying information to justify decisions; assessing evidence to formulate opinions.

Pupils will be able to
- provide a reason for black slaves escaping to Florida
- explain reasons behind chosen actions
- explore and evaluate historical attitudes towards different cultures.

Starter
Back-to-back: This provides a non-threatening way of getting pupils engaged in the lesson quickly, and provokes discussion in class. To debrief, encourage pupils to pick out things that they believe are key to understanding the image of an Indian before focusing on differences. Pupils can then write their own questions as to how and why there are differences, the basis of a useful 'hook' for the rest of the lesson.

Development
Green task: Pupils will be able to identify the origin of black Seminoles from source material on page 87 of *History in Progress – Book 2*. There is an obvious opportunity to examine slavery as a principle and the nature of life on a plantation. Turning the question around and asking pupils to describe the emotions and attitudes of the slave owners to safe harbours for runaway slaves starts the process that is picked up in later tasks.

Blue task: Pupils evaluate the way of life for slaves that have joined the Seminoles. With many sources here, the device of a secret message can be used to control length of exercise and method. A debrief should focus on the key factors for life with the Seminoles rather than just that slaves regained their freedom. As a comparison, refer to **Source c,** where 'free' slaves were still under an obligation.

Orange task: There is an option to develop the task as a genuine 'hot seat' conversation between three pupils, with a fourth recording the main points or formulating questions to challenge them. A debrief can focus on who's view had the strongest justification and why, a theme used in later lessons.

Plenary
'Killer' question: Pupils develop an open question which will elicit an answer of more than five words to test the understanding of other members of the group. Peer-assessment against simple criteria will promote engagement especially in areas of speaking and listening.

ICT opportunities
Task 3 can be completed as a digital video. Pupils can view the playback and assess the arguments.

History in Progress - LiveText CD 2: electronic activity

2.4 Why did the American Indians move west?

2.4c Andrew Jackson: hero or villain?

Learning objectives
- To be able to compare and contrast differing historical accounts.
- To use sources to reach a judgement as to the actions of Andrew Jackson.

Historical background
While George Washington and Abraham Lincoln are familiar to many people, President Andrew Jackson is less well known. A successful man of action, he lead US Army actions against the Creek Indians and the British in New Orleans. His achievements led him to be recognised as a national hero by Congress and he was Governor of Florida before becoming president in 1829. Yet it is Jackson's actions against the Seminole and other tribes that overshadow his accomplishments in the eyes of his critics today.

Teaching Activities and Learning Outcomes

Assessment opportunity
Interpreting sources and attributing characteristics to a historical character; reaching valid judgements.

Pupils will be able to
- select source material to produce a specific historical viewpoint
- explain how sources contribute to differing historical viewpoints
- reach validated judgements on a historical figure.

Starter
Money, money, money!: Pupils consider why someone would be put on a banknote as the way in to making a judgement about whether someone is a hero or villain. An obvious extension to the exercise would be to consider other people and their claim to fame before looking in detail at Andrew Jackson.

Development
Green task: This exercise will not be easy for some pupils whose role models are not easily accessible to everyone, and for whom a villain is someone from a film. The comparison of diagrams should highlight additional features, while by purposely asking pupils to remove parts of their answer, they are starting the process of selecting and prioritising that will focus their conclusions more sharply.

Blue task: The sources on pages 91-92 of *History in Progress – Book 2* can be pared down either for the purpose of differentiation or to achieve different types of reports. **Sources f** and **g** give a pro-Jackson 'spin' to the previous sources. The four sources in the next part of the task can be pre-determined by the teacher, but insisting on the inclusion of **f** and **g** 'as the views of the public' raises questions about how a prominent person is portrayed. From this, questions of validity can be raised.

Orange task: The focus should be on the new information and what it adds to our overall picture of Jackson. The activity could be conducted as a whole-class debate, before asking pupils to judge Jackson in light of all of the evidence. As a development of this phase of the lesson, pupils can link each source with either the hero or villain side of the spider diagram, before reaching a conclusion.

Plenary
Billboard: Pupils design a billboard poster for a film of Andrew Jackson to encourage them to think how such a 'Jekyll and Hyde' character might be portrayed. It also helps them to formulate their judgements.

Cross curricular links
Citizenship: Examining public figures and how they appear to the public – and whether this matters.

ICT opportunities
History in Progress - LiveText CD 2: electronic activity

Why did the American Indians move west?

2.4d What was the 'Trail of Tears'?

Learning objectives
- To be able to find out what was happening to other Indian tribes.
- To look at the significance of the 'Trail of Tears'.

Historical background
President Jackson's policies, specifically the 1830 Removal Act, sought to identify new lands for the incumbent tribes, so as to avoid further conflicts. This would directly lead to the 'Trail of Tears', the forced removal of the Cherokee nation to 'Indian Country' during the 1830s during which hundreds died.

Teaching Activities and Learning Outcomes

Assessment opportunity

Using source information to describe and explain motivation; selecting and presenting historical information within a context; reaching conclusions as to the significance of a historical event

Pupils will be able to

- produce a contextually accurate account of the events of the 'Trail of Tears'
- identify the significance of the 'Trail of Tears'.

Starter

Source a on page 94 of *History in Progress – Book 2* was painted 100 years after the event, something pupils may pick up on as they look at it. A useful technique is to divide the image into quarters so that pupils can focus on specific detail before reporting back to the group. Pupils should be encouraged to pick out similarity and anomaly in the painting before explaining what they think was happening overall.

Development

Why white settlers would have wanted land occupied by Indians at all can be explored generically in terms of 'What would you do?' which can provide an understanding of the options available.

Green task: It may be necessary to work through **source b** using practical examples of what each point would mean to those affected before setting the task. A development can be a quick survey as to whether the group feels President Jackson's actions were correct and why.

Blue task: As a means of differentiation/personalisation, pupils could be allocated only certain sources. An alternative task might be to pick out **sources g** and **i** (from Private Burnett) and write a diary from his point of view. To debrief, the focus can be on what was happening to the Cherokee and reflecting back on Jackson's motivation. Before the final task, attention should be drawn to the importance of the 'Manifest destiny' quote. This one quote provides a context for later Indian removals.

Orange task: To add a challenge to the task, pupils could be asked to do this in a dispassionate manner, using selected facts to explain the significance of the 'Trail of Tears' to the Cherokee nation. Pupils can then consider the original painting in light of further evidence before a final survey of opinion.

Plenary

Pupils could summarise the lesson/unit using a thinking skills triangle: the 'big idea' of the lesson put at the top, three key points beneath it and three specific details that add to the key points at the base.

ICT opportunities

Source a could be displayed on an electronic whiteboard using the Livetext Resource Bank. The toolbar allows aspects of the picture to be masked or highlighted.

History in Progress - LiveText CD 2: electronic activity

2.5: How did British industry change with new technology?

2.5a The significance of the steam engine

Learning objectives

- To explore how British industry changed with the invention of new technology.
- To assess the impact / significance of the invention of the steam engine to the Industrial Revolution.

Historical background

In 1698 Thomas Savery invented a steam engine that would pump water out of mines. In 1706 Thomas Newcomen improved this design. However, this was slow and expensive, and huge amounts of coal had to be used. In 1765 James Watt improved the steam engine further but did not have the money to make the precision parts needed for efficiency. Watt went into partnership with Matthew Boulton, and in 1775 the first Boulton and Watt engine was built. The foreman at their factory, William Murdock, developed the machine further so that it could be used to power any machines rather than a simple pumping motion.

Teaching Activities and Learning Outcomes

Assessment opportunity

Judging the historical significance of the invention of the steam engine.

Pupils will be able to

- identify the advantages of the steam engine to the cotton industry from a contemporary source
- assess the significance of the steam engine with regard to rate of introduction
- begin to analyse the success criteria used to judge significance.

Starter

Using **Worksheet 2.5a(i)**, pupils sort the cards into chronological order. This introduces the historical development of the steam engine and also helps pupils to understand the significance of the different individuals involved in its development.

Development

Green task: Pupils identify advantages of the steam engine to the cotton industry using a contemporary source. These are recorded on an ideas map. This can generate thoughts and a discussion on the disadvantages of water power and public opinion of the new invention.

Blue task: Using a table comparing water horsepower and steam horsepower in 1835 and a graph showing the relative trends of power and hand looms – pupils to describe trends then consider the speed/progress of the application of the invention. With this in mind they can then make a tentative judgement on its significance in history. This is a difficult thought provoking task challenging pupils to judge significance based on just one criteria – speed of take up.

Orange task: Pupils establish criteria they could use to judge an invention as significant, e.g.: 'uptake rapid'; 'uptake massive'; 'impacted on huge number of areas'; 'speeded up processes'; 'changed industry forever', etc. The criteria must then be applied to their knowledge of the steam engine, allowing them to judge the significance of the steam engine for themselves.

Plenary

The class compare the significance of the steam engine with a modern invention of their own choice and explain the parallel they have drawn. This consolidates the concept of criteria to judge significance.

ICT opportunities

History in Progress - LiveText CD 2: electronic activity

2.5 How did British industry change with new technology?

Worksheet 2.5a(i) The invention of the steam engine

Thomas Savery invented a steam engine to pump water from mines. However, it had no safety valve.

James Watt improved Newcomen's steam engine further but did not have the money or expertise to make precision parts.

Thomas Newcomen improved the design of the original engine by attaching a beam to operate pumps in mines. However, it was slow and expensive and used huge amounts of coal.

Watt went into partnership with Matthew Boulton, who could build the precision parts. They built the first Boulton and Watt Engine, but still only provided up and down motion.

William Murdock invented the sun and planet gear, which finally allowed the steam engine to power all sorts of machines.

Timeline for the invention of the steam engine

| 1698 | 1706 | | 1765 | 1775 | 1781 |

2.5 How did British industry change with new technology?

Worksheet 2.5a(ii) What advantages did steam power have?

Using **source a** on page 98 of *History in Progress – Book 2*, complete the ideas map below to show the advantages of the steam engine for the cotton industry compared to water power.

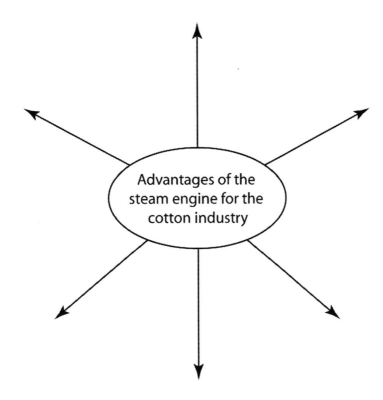

2.5 How did British industry change with new technology?

2.5b Reaction to the new technology

Learning objectives
- To examine the impact of the introduction of new technology.
- To examine and evaluate the reaction of these workers to the introduction of new technology.

Historical background
Seven hundred full-scale riots took place in Britain between 1790 and 1840. During this time, new machines were able to do work previously done by men, women and children, whose services were no longer required. It was from these workers that many of the rioters came. From 1811 to 1816 weavers, wool combers and others resorted to smashing up the new machinery. They became known as Luddites, led by the fictional Ned Lud.

Teaching activities and learning outcomes:

Assessment opportunity
Examining the impact of technological change on workers and their reactions to the changes.

Pupils will be able to
- analyse the declining trend in handloom weavers and the increasing trend in power looms
- examine the correlation data relating to the industrial revolution
- write a letter from Ned Lud justifying the actions of the Luddites and their militant behaviour.

Starter
Using **Worksheet 2.5b** pupils compare **sources a** and **b** of modern-day protests, and think about which form of protest is more effective and why. This introduces them to the topic of public protest and encourages them to think about why groups chose to riot to gain attention for their cause.

Development
Green task: Pupils analyse data, and examine trends and pace of change, and explain any anomalies. Next, they should empathise and assess how the introduction of new technology would have been viewed by a factory owner and by a worker. More able pupils should begin to question which worker – if they were a machine worker, then they would benefit.

Blue task: Pupils identify relationships between the rising price of corn, the declining wages of the handloom weavers and the incidence of riots. They are to agree or disagree with majority government opinion at the time that the Luddites were a well-oiled political faction attempting to overthrow the ruling classes behind the facade of oppressed workers. This gives pupils the opportunity to consider how interpretations of events differ according to perspective.

Orange task: This task is made more challenging by asking pupils to consider how they can justify the actions of the Luddites trying to protect the jobs of the workers, yet at the same time, forcing the machine workers into the same oppressed state as themselves. This high order thinking activity may demand pupils to reconsider how the Luddites' tactics did not always match their objectives.

Plenary
Discuss it: Do the advantages of the introduction of machinery outweigh the disadvantages? Draw out from pupils that it would depend on who you were – factory owner, handloom weaver, machine worker.

ICT opportunities
History in Progress – LiveText CD 2: electronic activity

2.5 How did British industry change with the new technology?

Worksheet 2.5b Reactions to the new technology

Source a

Source b

Look at **sources a** and **b**, then answer these questions.

- Why do you think groups of people choose to protest?
- What differences can you see in the way that people have chosen to protest?
- Which type of protest do you think would be the most effective in getting its message across?
- Which type of protest would be the most effective if it wanted media coverage?

2.5: How did British industry change with new technology?

2.5c What was the cost to women?

Learning objectives
- To understand the consequences of the Industrial Revolution with regard to the role of women.
- To suggest different reasons for interpretations of the past.

Historical background
During the Industrial Revolution some traditional jobs for women, such as domestic spinning, replaced by new jobs such as carding. In fact the proportion of women at work in the nineteenth century was probably no larger then earlier. However, their work was largely unskilled and paid lower wages than men; additionally, the work was neither regular nor secure.

Teaching Activities and Learning Outcomes

Assessment opportunity

Recognising and describing nature of diversity; recognising some reasons for different interpretations.

Pupil will be able to

- prepare a speech for parliament highlighting conditions of working women using sources
- evaluate and tabulate suggested intentions for why sources were written
- analyse different contemporary opinions of women towards their condition.

Starter

Using **Worksheet 2.5c**, pupils should match the increase or decrease to the correct occupation, which should generate a discussion about causation and consequence.

Development

- **Green task:** Using **sources a–d** from page 102-103 of *History in Progress – Book 2*, pupils prepare a parliamentary speech highlighting the working conditions, treatment and rates of pay of women. This will develop their ability to extract and deploy relevant information from sources.
- **Blue task:** Using **source b** by Lord Shaftsbury, pupils evaluate the intention of the author. This is an essential skill to develop in order to analyse sources fully. It forces pupils to consider motivation behind the reforms and to appreciate attitudes of the period.
- **Orange task:** Pupils empathise with why some women would not have wanted reform. They should consider the reduction in family wages and blocking the entry of women into certain heavy trades. More able pupils may equate modern concepts of feminism to some complaints against reform. Pupils should consider the reliability and/or usefulness of government enquiries/commissions as evidence of working conditions. More able pupils will question the selection of witnesses and the motivations of male MPs.

Plenary

Class discussion and final vote: Should working conditions be reformed? Those completing various levels of task could give layered contributions giving depth to the equality of rights of women discussion.

Cross-curricular links

Citizenship: similarities between these conditions and conditions in the world in the present day.

ICT opportunities

History in Progress – LiveText CD 2: electronic activity

2.5 How did British industry change with new technology?

Worksheet 2.5c The cost to women

Match the type of industry to the numbers of people working in it.

Which industries increased? Which decreased?

Agriculture, Farming	1851–229,000 1911–117,000
Textile cloth making in the factories	1851–635,000 1991–870,000
Metal making in the factories	1851–36,000 1911–128,000

2.5 How did British industry change with new technology?

2.5d Taking it further!: The 'Great' Exhibition: did everyone agree?

Learning objectives
- To interpret the reality of the Great Exhibition from a range of social contexts.
- To reflect critically on a historical event evaluating sources to reach reasoned conclusions.

Historical background
The Great Exhibition opened in May 1851 and was a celebration of Britain's industrial and technological supremacy. In total there were about six million visitors to the Crystal Palace during the Exhibition including many working class people, although they were encouraged to visit on special 'shilling days' so that they did not mix with the upper classes.

Teaching Activities and Learning Outcomes

Assessment opportunity

Evaluating whether the Great Exhibition as a display of Britain's economic wealth and domination, actually reflected the reality for all classes of society.

Pupils will be able to

- describe the Great Exhibition from a British and from a foreign perspective as an advertising leaflet
- assess the impact of the Great Exhibition on mixing of the social classes
- assess the impact of technological and industrial development on the poor compared to the rich.

Starter

Pupils list ten 'great' inventions of their time and discuss what makes them great. Use this to introduce concepts of 'advancement' and 'wealth' as features of 'great' inventions. It can also lead to a discussion of the size of inventions now and how they could be displayed compared to those of 160 years ago.

Development

- **Task 1:** This task consolidates the concept of Britain as 'workshop of the world' at this time. Victorians saw bringing British goods and British values to 'less civilised' nations as one of their greatest achievements.
- **Task 2:** Pupils interpret the message of the cartoonist in **source c** on page 104 of *History in Progress – Book 2*. More able pupils should make social comments on how the poor, the worker bees, should remain unseen. They were not to be a visible part of the Great Exhibition in any way.
- **Task 3:** Pupils use the opinion of a contemporary socialist to assess the importance of the very technology the Great Exhibition showed off to the world on the poor.

Plenary

Pupils discuss two key questions. In their opinion did the Great Exhibition reflect the reality of being the 'workshop of the world'? If it had reflected the true reality of being the 'workshop of the world' what would public reaction then have been? Would the rich have even visited?

Cross-curricular links

Technology, engineering, citizenship

ICT opportunities

Research the structure of Crystal Palace. What happened to it when it was taken down? What was the 'Battle of the Elms', which was directly caused by Prince Albert's idea for the building of Crystal Palace? *History in Progress LIveText CD 2:* electronic activity

2.6 What was it like to be poor in nineteenth-century Britain?

2.6a Life in the workhouse

Learning objectives
- To investigate conditions in workhouses.
- To understand why the workhouses were set up and judge whether their conditions were too harsh on the poor.

Historical background
Workhouses were set up to provide accommodation, food and work for the very poor. Workhouses had been around since the sixteenth century, but were only built on a large scale after the Poor Law of 1834. According to this law, workhouses were to provide the main method of help for the poor; other methods such as charitable handouts were not encouraged because it was felt they cultivated laziness among the poor. It was widely believed that poverty was primarily the fault of the poor themselves. The workhouse regime was deliberately harsh to discourage the poor to look for charity there. As a result only the most desperate tended to seek help in the workhouse.

Teaching Activities and Learning Outcomes

Homework
Researching further sources that provide evidence of conditions in workhouses.

Pupils will be able to
- select information from sources to make judgements about conditions in workhouses
- write a report which organises and explains the main points about the conditions in the workhouses
- explain why there were different interpretations about the effectiveness of workhouses.

Starter
Encourage pupils to think about what help is provided for the poor today. Pupils might suggest: pensions, adoption, foster care, child support, welfare benefit, housing assistance, insurance payments for sickness or injury.

Development
Green task: This could be a paired activity to encourage discussion of the worst features of the workhouse.

Blue task: Encourage pupils to organise their report on workhouse conditions under the headings recommended and to support their points with evidence. This could perhaps be extended as an ICT task with pupils designing their report with illustrations, interviews and further research. **Worksheet 2.6a** supports this task.

Orange task: Encourage pupils to appreciate different points of view about the effectiveness of the workhouse system.

Plenary
Reflect back on the **starter** and encourage pupils to think about why provision for the poor has changed so much. Pupils will probably highlight how beliefs about why people are poor have changed.

Cross-curricular links
Citizenship: The extent of the responsibilities of the state for the welfare of the poor.

ICT opportunities
History in Progress - LiveText CD 2: electronic activity

2.6 What was it like to be poor in nineteenth-century Britain?

Worksheet 2.6a Life in the workhouse

Imagine you are an inspector who has visited several workhouses and has been asked to write a report on the conditions and treatment of the paupers.

a) Complete this spider diagram of what your report will cover.

| Food |

| Workhouse conditions |

| Living conditions |

| Work |

| Punishments |

b) Give your verdict about whether you think the conditions were too harsh.

_____

_____

_____

_____

2.6 What was it like to be poor in nineteenth-century Britain?

2.6b Poor children

Learning objectives
- To discover the ways in which life was difficult for poor children in the nineteenth century.
- To understand the changes which took place to help poor children and how far this helped them.

Historical background
Poverty was a significant problem during the Victorian period. The government gave the poor little help except for the workhouse which was so harsh that few wanted to enter it. The poor had to rely instead on charity. Unfairly, it was widely believed that poverty was the fault of the poor themselves, attributed to laziness, drink or crime. Children could be plunged into poverty through the death of their parents (like Oliver Twist) and found themselves forced to earn a living through selling things on the streets. Dr Barnardo established his charity, Barnardos in 1868 to provide shelter for homeless children in London.

Teaching Activities and Learning Outcomes

Assessment opportunity
Extended explanation about the problems of poor children in the nineteenth century, recognising change and continuity in the amount of help provided to them.

Pupils will be able to
- select information from sources as evidence of the problems of poor children
- recognise change and continuity in the amount of help provided to poor children
- write an extended explanation on the problems of child poverty in the nineteenth century.

Starter
Look at **source a** (from *Oliver Twist*) and the question on page 108 of *History in Progress – Book 2*. Pupils might have prior knowledge of Oliver Twist, which could be the basis of a discussion about what they already know about how life was hard for poor children in the nineteenth century.

Development
Green task: Pupils select information from **sources b-d** to fill in **Worksheet 2.6b**. Tasks 1b and 1c could be discussion-based activities.
Blue task: Encourage pupils to think about changes in help provided to poor children.

Orange task: Pupils can create an extended piece of writing, as a speech or pamphlet explaining the problems of child poverty and identifying the changes made. They should be encouraged to structure their explanation under the headings suggested and support their points with evidence.

Plenary
Time for reflection: Ask pupils to consider how different life was for children in the nineteenth century compared with today. Pupils should make two suggestions to a partner.

Cross-curricular links
Citizenship: The responsibilities of the state to provide for children in poverty.

ICT opportunities
History in Progress – LiveText CD 2: electronic activity

2.6 What was it like to be poor in nineteenth-century Britain?

Worksheet 2.6b Poor children

1a) Complete this table using **sources b–d** from page 108 of *History in Progress – Book 2* to record the details of work done by children in the nineteenth century.

	Flower seller	**Mudlark**	**Factory girl**
Age?			
How much money did they make on average a day?			
Did they have parents? Did their parents work?			
Were they educated?			
Did their work affect their health?			

b) Choose one of the children and identify the main reasons why the work they did was tiring and dangerous?

_____

_____

_____

_____

c) Suggest changes that could have been made to improve the working life of the child you described in task 1b.

_____

_____

_____

_____

2.7 How did urban life change in the nineteenth century?

2.7a Growth of the cities

Learning objectives
- To understand the reasons why towns grew in size in the nineteenth century, and with what results.
- To weigh up the advantages and disadvantages of the rapid growth of towns.

Historical background
Urbanisation was one of the greatest changes to take place in the nineteenth century. The census of 1851 revealed that for the first time more than 50% of the population lived in towns. The greatest growth occurred in London and the new industrial towns in the north like Manchester and Sheffield, which grew up as a result of the industrial revolution. The consequences of this rapid growth were both positive and negative – the negative focusing on over-crowded housing, poverty and crime.

Teaching Activities and Learning Outcomes

Assessment opportunity
Explaining the changes that took place in towns.

Pupils will be able to
- suggest five reasons why people moved to towns and cities
- create a spider diagram to show consequences of the growth of towns
- write a letter describing life in the towns and cities.

Starter
Ask pupils to suggest reasons for urbanisation in the 19th century. This could be a discussion-based activity. Pupils suggestions may include: the discovery of resources, trade, factory centres, famine.

Development
Green task: Pupils identify reasons why people moved to towns. In discussion, encourage them to think about the consequences of such rapid and large-scale migration.

Blue task: Pupils identify the main consequences of growth in the size of towns by creating a spider diagram. The identification of positive and negative consequences could be undertaken in pairs or as a class discussion.

Orange task: This allows for a more extended explanation picking up on recognising the changes that occurred in towns and the positive and negative consequences of these changes.

Plenary
Snowballing: Pupils suggest one advantage and one disadvantage of living in towns in the nineteenth century, then join with another pair, then another group, to share their ideas. Ask pupils to reflect on whether they think the advantages and disadvantages of living there, are the same today as they were in the nineteenth century.

Cross-curricular links
Citizenships: The problems (and advantages) of urbanisation.

ICT opportunities
History in Progress – LiveText CD 2: electronic activity

2.7 How did urban life change in the nineteenth century?

2.7b Public health

Learning objectives
- To find out about what public healthcare was like in nineteenth-century Darlington.
- To weigh up how much public health in improved in Darlington in the nineteenth century.

Historical background
Disease was relatively common in the nineteenth century and particularly feared was cholera. The reasons why disease was so common had much to do with poor living conditions in urban centres where overcrowding and poor sanitation provision were a consequence of the mass, rapid urbanisation of the nineteenth century. The government was spurred on by a number of serious epidemics to take action to improve public healthcare. One of the most tragic was the cholera outbreak in Soho in London in 1854 in which more than 600 people died as the result of a cesspit leaking into the freshwater pump.

Teaching Activities and Learning Outcomes

Assessment opportunity

Identifying and explaining change and continuity in public healthcare provision.

Pupils will be able to

- complete a table to show public health problems and solutions
- suggest arguments for and against the Public Health Board
- write a speech explaining achievements made in public health and work still to be done.

Starter

Gimme 5: In pairs pupils suggest five measures that are used to maintain the hygiene of towns today. Pupils may suggest: bins, refuse collection, good sewage and drainage, fresh drinking water, etc.

Development

Green task: Pupils use the information on pages 112-113 of *History in Progress – Book 2* to identify the threats to public health in Darlington and the measures taken in the nineteenth century to improve the situation in order to fill in the table. **Worksheet 2.7b** supports this task.

Blue task: Pupils identify the main complaints against government intervention to improve public health and then formulate a government response to these complaints. This task could be anticipated by a discussion of who may complain about the reforms that had been made in Darlington and why. Pupils will probably highlight the cost as a likely issue of complaint.

Orange task: Remind pupils that their speech needs to be convincing and persuasive. They should explain clearly what has been done so far, what still needs to be done and counter any arguments against the Board. Work from tasks 1 and 2 builds up to this task. On completion, pupils can read their speeches to each other. There is also the opportunity for some peer review.

Plenary

Think, pair, share: Pupils discuss how changes in public healthcare in the nineteenth century anticipated modern provision. Make links back to the ideas suggested in the starter.

Cross-curricular links

Citizenship and science: The extent and quality of healthcare provided to citizens.

ICT opportunities

History in Progress – LiveText CD 2: electronic activity

2.7 How did urban life change during the nineteenth century?

Worksheet 2.7b Public health

1   Select information from pages 112-113 of *History in Progress – Book 2* to show the problems to health relating to housing, water and waste, then record them in the appropriate column below.

Issue	The problems in 1849	Action taken to improve health
Housing		
Water		
Waste		

2   Imagine you are a member of the Board of Health. What five measures would you recommend the Board introduce to help solve these problems?

_____

_____

_____

3   Select information from **source b** which shows the changes introduced in Darlington to improve housing, water and waste, then record them in the last column on your table. How many of these recommendations match the ones you made?

_____

_____

_____

_____

_____

_____

2.7 How did urban life change in the nineteenth century?

2.7c Life in nineteenth-century London

Learning objectives
- To find out what Victorian London was like.
- To identify ways in which transport and entertainment changed, and judge whether the changes were improvements.

Historical background
In the Victorian period London expanded significantly and was modernised through the building of railways, underground railways, sewage systems, street lights and modern entertainments. However, in many ways Victorian London remained an old-fashioned city, with areas of slum housing, animals in the streets and horse-drawn vehicles as the main method of transport.

Teaching Activities and Learning Outcomes

Assessment opportunity

Identifying change and continuity to London's transport and entertainment in the nineteenth century.

Pupils will be able to

- create a timeline to show change and continuity in nineteenth-century London
- write a postcard describing London in 1890 and how it has changed
- draw comparisons between transport and entertainment in Victorian and modern times.

Starter

Ask pupils to give their impressions of London in 1872 from **source a** (the Gustav Dore drawing) on page 114 of *History in Progress – Book 2*. Pupils will probably notice that the drawing shows a combination of modern developments like the steam train, and more old-fashioned aspects such as the flock of sheep being taken to market and the horse-drawn buses.

Development

Green task: Pupils complete their own timeline to develop an understanding of chronology in identifying changes to London. This could be followed by a discussion asking pupils to consider if all the changes were improvements, which will provide links with task 3.

Blue task: Pupils must first show an understanding of what London was like and the opportunities there were for people in 1890 in terms of entertainment and transport by planning a day out. Then they write a postcard to show how London had changed during the nineteenth century. Pupils can use the timeline created in task 1 to help them with this.

Orange task: This could take the form of a group discussion, with each group nominating a spokesperson to feedback to the class.

Plenary

Three things: Pupils list what they think were the three most important changes to towns they have learned about in this enquiry. They should compare their list with a partner and discuss any differences.

ICT opportunities

History in Progress – LiveText CD 2: electronic activity

2.7 How did urban life change in the nineteenth century?

2.7d Taking it further!: Sun, sea and sand: getting out of the towns

Learning objectives
- To use source material to explain the significance of the changes the railway brought to urban dwellers.

Historical background
For many ordinary people the railway brought opportunities that could only have been dreamed of in the eighteenth century. The freedom of movement brought by the train was enhanced by legislation that enshrined the principle of leisure time. This combination ushered in the golden age of British seaside resorts, as they become 'worker's playgrounds'. Nowhere was this more true than of Blackpool, located as it was close to the industrial populations of Lancashire and now accessible to people further afield.

Teaching Activities and Learning Outcomes

Assessment opportunity
Using source material to assess the nature of change.

Pupils will be able to
- use sources to establish their importance in understanding how the railway contributed to change.

Starter
Pupils review **source a** (an advert) on page 116 of *History in Progress – Book 2* and have their attention drawn to specific features. The text is important to the whole image, and one method of focusing pupils on the message would be to cover the text to begin with. Pupils could be asked to pick out the message of the poster and who it might appeal to before addressing the purpose.

Development
The 5Ws: This can provide a way to access the questions about how individuals felt about going to Blackpool. Identifying the differences between the responses to the activity and why they occurred may give the support needed to develop a deeper understanding of how the world was changing, and the role of the railway in that change. To help consolidate learning, ask pupils to 'bridge' their understanding of how the railway was bringing about change to different scenarios that existed at the time.

The challenge posed by the review of individual opinions highlights the problem of dealing with differing perspectives. An oral exercise where pupils present the opinion of their 'talking heads' will provide an opportunity to reflect on their own interpretation of the sources, and allow pupils to raise questions of interpretation.

The final question could be posed in 'Devil's Advocate' form, asking to what extent the railway brought about change or whether it was in response to the change in society.

Plenary
Time for reflection: Ask pupils to think about all the sources in this enquiry. Pupils should each provide one reason, backed up by these sources, why a holiday in Blackpool would have been better than life at home for a worker. This may include reasons to do with health or leisure.

ICT opportunities
Using the masking feature from the Livetext CD-ROM resource bank, enlarge the Blackpool advert on an electronic whiteboard, which will enable pupils to break down different aspects of the picture.

History in Progress – LiveText CD 2: electronic activity

2.8 What was law and order like during the eighteenth and nineteenth centuries?

2.8a How did law and order change?

Learning objectives
- To find out what law and order was like during the eighteenth and nineteenth centuries.
- To explain how law and order changed during the eighteenth and nineteenth centuries.

Historical background
Law and order in industrialised Britain had changed very little since medieval times. However, the increase in population during the Industrial Revolution also led to an increase in crime. Over 200 crimes were punishable by the death penalty but this did not seem to deter criminals in the way the authorities had hoped. There were no police, no system of courts or suitable punishments such as imprisonment, and things were becoming difficult to manage. During the nineteenth century this began to change.

Teaching Activities and Learning Outcomes

Homework

Pupils research one form of punishment from the eighteenth or nineteenth centuries and feed back to the whole class next lesson. Punishments could include: transportation, crank handle, treadwheel.

Pupils will be able to

- rank changes to law and order in order of importance
- write a short newspaper article either for or against the prison system, including a headline
- write a report about prisons in 1858 from the point of view of a prison inspector.

Starter

Pupils study **source f** on page 121 of *History in Progress – Book 2*. What do they think is happening in the picture and why? What do they think was the purpose of the punishment? Would it be successful in deterring people from re-offending? Why? Why not? How does it compare to punishment today?

Development

Green task: Working in pairs and using the timeline on page 118, pupils rank the changes that took place in law and order. They should explain clearly why they have ranked the changes in the order that they have. Some pupils may struggle with this, so you might want to give them an example of ranking. For task 1b pupils explain their rankings clearly to another pair and listen to their explanations. Once discussions have taken place, groups may want to reorder their changes again.

Blue task: Working in pairs pupils write a short argument either in favour of or against the new prison systems. Then they design a newspaper headline and front page based on the argument they have written. These could form a classroom display and offer the opportunity for peer-assessment.

Orange task: Pupils write a report ensuring that they include the changes made to prisons, effects on prisoners and what further improvements they could make.

Plenary

Pupils design their own form of punishment which they feel would be more appropriate and effective than the existing ones in the eighteenth and nineteenth centuries.

ICT opportunities

History in Progress – LiveText CD 2: electronic activity

2.8 What was law and order like during the eighteenth and nineteenth centuries?

2.8b Were Britain's first policemen popular?

Learning objectives
- To understand the role of the Metropolitan police from 1829 onwards.
- To use sources to find out what people thought of the new police force at the time.

Historical background
Law and order in Great Britain had not changed greatly since medieval times, but as the population rose more people were committing crimes. This led to many middle class people in London worrying about who would prevent and solve crimes, as the watchmen were not efficient enough. In 1829 the prime minister, Sir Robert Peel, created the Metropolitan Police Force in London, but it was not always respected by the London population.

Teaching Activities and Learning Outcomes

Assessment

Tasks 2 and 3: evaluating sources to reach reasoned conclusions about what people thought of the police force at the time.

Pupils will be able to

- identify skills and equipment required by policemen in the nineteenth century
- use sources to find out more about the contemporary view of the police force.

Starter

Pupils suggest the different duties that modern-day police officers are expected to do and what skills they need to do a good job. How are police officers regarded today? This might be an emotive issue, so the discussion should be managed carefully with pupils being clear about what is and is not acceptable.

Development

Green task: Pupils use information from **source a** on page 122 of *History in Progress – Book 2* to establish skills required by a nineteenth-century policeman. Then they use the information and their own knowledge to rank these.

Blue task: Pupils study **source b**, which provides another point of view about the reputation of the police force. Reinforce that cartoons often exaggerate certain characteristics to make a point. How far do pupils think they can trust this source?

Orange task: Pupils examine the purpose, origin and nature of the sources in this lesson in order to learn about contemporary opinions of the police in the mid-nineteenth century. A recap of the 5Ws is included on page 182 to help pupils with this task.

Plenary

Back to the start: Pupils suggest one thing that nineteenth-century policemen had in common with modern-day officers and one thing that is different.

Cross-curricular links

Citizenship: The law and order aspect of this lesson and the development of the police force in Great Britain falls under the remit of KS3 Citizenship.

ICT opportunities

History in Progress – LiveText CD 2: electronic activity

2.8 What was law and order like during the eighteenth and nineteenth centuries?

2.8c Taking it further!: Catching Jack the Ripper!

Learning objectives

- To use contemporary evidence as part of an enquiry.

Historical background

Jack the Ripper was the name given to a serial killer who murdered several prostitutes in the East End of London in 1888. The name comes from a letter written by someone who claimed to be the killer published at the time of the murders. The true identity of the Ripper has never been confirmed, though there were at the time and have been since a number of suspects. The killings took place within a one mile area in the districts of Whitechapel, Spitalfields, Aldgate, and the City of London.

Teaching Activities and Learning Outcomes

Homework

Pupils design their own wanted poster from 1888 using the information from the lesson to describe the type of suspect they are looking for.

Pupils will be able to

- produce a table of evidence outlining what it tells them about the case
- write a report explaining the problems the police had in solving the murders.

Starter

As a class, pupils discuss different methods used by the police today to catch a murderer. This should be brainstormed on the board.

Development

- **Task 1:** Pupils examine **sources a–e** on pages 124-125 of *History in Progress – Book 2* in order to make informed decisions about the sources and complete **Worksheet 2.8c**. Ensure you encourage pupils to explain why they have sorted the evidence in the way they have.
- **Task 2:** Once pupils have completed the worksheet, they should use the information from it to write a report explaining why they believe the police could not solve the Whitechapel murders in 1888. Emphasise that pupils must back up their suggestions with information from the sources. Go through the sentence structures to give them guidance with their writing.

Plenary

Think, pair, share: pupils suggest what they think was the biggest change in law and order during the eighteenth and nineteenth centuries. Remind them that they need to be able to justify their decision. Take feedback from the groups.

ICT opportunities

History in Progress – LiveText CD 2: electronic activity on Jack the Ripper

2.8c What was law and order like during the eighteenth and nineteenth centuries?

Worksheet 2.8c Jack the Ripper: evidence

Use **sources a–e** on pages 124-125 of *History in Progress – Book 2* to complete the table below. Make sure you think carefully about why you are sorting your evidence in this way.

Source	What it says about the identity of the 'Ripper'	What it says about the problems the police might have had solving the case
a		
b		
c		
d		
e		

Once you have completed the table, highlight any similarities you can see between what the sources are saying.

Unit 2 Living and working

2.9 Making connections: Country swap

Learning objectives
- To discover the differences between two different cultures.
- To use modern-day media skills to present historical information.

Historical background
Life changed greatly from the seventeenth to the nineteenth centuries in Britain as well as all around the rest of the world. The Industrial Revolution brought great changes to the lifestyle of people living in Britain. Some of these changes were for the better and some made people's lives worse. However, while Britain became the 'workshop of the world', other countries such as China and America were making great leaps themselves, culturally, scientifically and artistically. While on the surface these three countries seem very different, a closer examination reveals that aspects of their lifestyles were similar. This lesson asks pupils to examine the similarities and differences.

Teaching Activities and Learning Outcomes

Assessment opportunity
Making links between different cultures throughout history.

Starter
Snowballing: Pupils work in pairs, then join with another pair, and another group, to share ideas on what they can remember about the different aspects of lifestyles for British, Chinese and American people during the period studied in this unit.

Development
- **Green task:** Working in pairs pupils plan an episode of a television show called 'Culture Swap'. They choose two of three cultures (Britain, China and America) to research and plan a television show storyboard. Pupils can use the storyboard templates on **Worksheet 2.9** to map out their storyboards and captions. They could also use the Internet to locate images for their storyboard. More able pairs should try to include more than the six suggested scenes in their storyboard.
- **Blue task:** Individually, pupils should write a 5-minute script for one of the countries. Once these scripts are complete, pupils can swap them with their partner and make suggestions for improvements. Emphasise that this peer review should offer positive criticism.
- **Orange task:** The last activity for the most able encourages them to write a review of their 'Culture Swap' episode.

Plenary
Storyboards are pinned around the classroom; a class vote decides which would deliver the best show.

Cross-curricular links
- **Citizenship**: Pupils are examining living conditions for three different cultures.
- **Media:** Using Media skills in a historical setting.

ICT opportunities
History in Progress – LiveText CD 2: electronic activity

Unit 2 Living and working

Worksheet 2.9 Country swap

Use the storyboard below to plan and produce your episode of the television show 'Culture Swap'.

Selected country: _____

Unit 2 Living and working

Assessment Unit 2

2.10 Assessment task 1: What were the most important changes in living conditions in Britain between 1603 and 1901?

Pupils will be able to

- explain the significance of events/inventions/people in history.

What the task is about

- First, pupils reflect on different aspects of improvements that they have learned about. Then they select the five most significant events and changes to Britain between the period 1603 and 1901.
- For each change pupils select, they need to demonstrate how people's lives changed for the better. For example, if a pupil selects the invention of trains, they should then describe in their summary how trains allowed people who worked in towns to travel to the seaside for holidays, which improved their lives by providing them with quality leisure time.
- Encourage the pupils to choose a mix of inventions and events. Remind them that people and political movements improved Britain just as much as inventions.
- Pupils should present their ideas as summaries of different sections or pages of a website. They might present each summary as a slide in a PowerPoint presentation or on an A5 piece of paper.
- Pupils will move up the different levels depending on the quality of the explanation for each event/invention/person that they choose.
- A markscheme is provided on **Worksheet 2.10a**.
- The assessment exercise should take place at the end of Unit 2 Living and working

2.11 Assessment task 2: Were pauper apprentices in nineteenth-century factories all treated the same?

Pupils will be able to

- interpret information as part of an enquiry.

What the task is about

- Explain that the focus of this assessment task is interpretation of sources. Ask pupils to read through page 130 of *History in Progress – Book 2*. They should examine each source, then answer the questions as they go along. Guidance for pupils on questions is provided on page 131; they might also find it useful to refer to the skills bank on pages 182-183.
- This task is supported by **Worksheet 2.11a**.
- The difficulty level increases as the questions progress.
- It is intended that pupils tackle these assessment tasks individually; less able pupils might benefit from discussing the tasks first as a whole class or in pairs.
- Pupils who complete all of the assessment tasks will find themselves progressing to Levels 4–6.
- A markscheme is provided on **Worksheet 2.11b**.
- This assessment task can be completed at the end of Unit 2 Living and working.

Unit 2 Assessment 1

Worksheet 2.10a What were the most important changes in living conditions in Britain between 1603 and 1901?

How did you do?

Level 4: I was able to …	
describe five key changes in nineteenth century Britain.	
say how each change was important.	
explain one way in which each change altered people's lives.	
Use dates and historical words correctly.	

Level 5: I was able to …	
describe five key changes in more detail and put them in the right time frame.	
select and use information to show why each change was important.	
explain how each change altered people's lives and made started to links between these.	
use the correct historical terms.	

Level 6: I was able to …	
describe in detail the different types of five changes that were taking place in Britain in the nineteenth century.	
show what criteria I used to decide which are the most important changes.	
explain how and why each change altered people's lives and make links between these.	
select, organise and use relevant information and the correct historical terms.	

Things I did well: _____

_____

I need to learn more about: _____

_____

One thing I need to improve is: _____

_____

I will do this by: _____

_____

Teacher comment: _____

Pupil comment: _____

Unit 2 Assessment 2

Worksheet 2.11a(i)

Were pauper apprentices in nineteenth-century factories all treated the same?

> a
>
> In the room they entered, the dirty, ragged miserable crew. Lean and distorted limbs – sallow and sunken cheeks – dim hollow eyes ... a look of hideous premature old age.

Extract from *Michael Armstrong, the Factory Boy* written by Frances Trollope, 1840. This book described working conditions for pauper apprentices.

1 What can you learn from **source a** about the health of pauper apprentices who worked in factories during the Industrial Revolution? Use the table below to record your ideas.

What source a suggests about the health of pauper apprentices	Quotes from source a to support this

Unit 2 Assessment 2

Worksheet 2.11a(ii)

Were pauper apprentices in nineteenth-century factories all treated the same?

2 Sources a and **b** on page 130 of *History in Progress – Book 2* give very different impressions of the way pauper apprentices were treated by factory owners. Use the tables below to record your ideas about each source.

Source a

What can I learn about how pauper apprentices were treated?	Who wrote the source?	Why might the source be reliable?	Why might the source be unreliable?

Source b

What can I learn about how pauper apprentices were treated?	Who wrote the source?	Why might the source be reliable?	Why might the source be unreliable?

a Is one of these sources wrong? Explain your answer: _____

_____

_____

b Which source do you think is more reliable? Why? _____

_____

_____

Unit 2 Assessment 2

Worksheet 2.11a(iii)

Were pauper apprentices in nineteenth-century factories all treated the same?

Look at **source c** on page 130 of *History in Progress – Book 2*. It was painted for a novel describing working conditions for pauper apprentices and shows children eating scraps from a pig's trough. Do you think **source c** best supports **source a** or **b**?

What does **source a** suggest about working conditions for children?	What does **source b** suggest about working conditions for children?	How does **source c** support **source a**?	How does **source c** support **source b**?

Source d was written by a modern historian. Does it agree or disagree with previous sources about how pauper apprentices were treated?

Some pauper apprentices worked in factories owned by caring factory owners. They were well fed, educated and taught a trade. Other children were unlucky and became cheap slave labour. They were often injured from the dangerous factory machinery.

a Explain how **source d** agrees with **sources a–c** about how pauper apprentices were treated?

_____

_____

_____

_____

_____

b Explain how **source d** disagrees with **sources a–c** about how pauper apprentices were treated?

_____

_____

_____

_____

Now use all the information you have gathered in this lesson to write an answer to the following question: Were pauper apprentices in nineteenth-century factories all treated the same?

Unit 2 Assessment 2

Worksheet 2.11b Were pauper apprentices in nineteenth-century factories all treated the same?

How did you do?

Level 4: I was able to …	
describe what life was like for the pauper apprentices, demonstrating that I can interpret information written at the time.	
show that I understand that people have different points of view about working conditions in the past.	
select the right information to answer the question appropriately, written in clear and simple sentences using the correct dates and historical terms.	

Level 5: I was able to …	
demonstrate that I understand how factories across Britain might treat pauper apprentices differently.	
suggest more than one reason why people in the past have different points of view about factory conditions.	
select the correct information to produce a well-structured answer.	

Level 6: I was able to …	
show that I understand how factories across Britain might treat pauper apprentices differently and why people at the time had such different opinions about working conditions.	
to suggest more than one reason why people in the past have different points of view about factory conditions and explain why all of these opinions are important.	
select and organise the correct information to best answer the question.	

Things I did well: _____

_____

I need to learn more about: _____

_____

One thing I need to improve is: _____

_____

I will do this by: _____

_____

Teacher comment: _____

Pupil comment: _____

3.1 What were the real reasons Britain wanted an empire?

3.1a Building the empire

Learning objectives
- To explore the effect of the growth of the British Empire on Britain and the colonies.
- To begin to explain relationships between causes of colonization.

Historical background
Throughout the nineteenth and the first half of the twentieth century, Britain had the largest empire in the world. The Empire increased for several reasons: British merchants were trading all over the world and British government wanted more control over the countries in which there were trading posts; missionaries were keen to convert people to Christianity; explorers wanted to discover and claim new lands; and the lands of the empire provided raw materials along with a ready workforce and if necessary troops. Above all, an empire was a symbol of power and competition to build empires grew in this period.

Teaching Activities and Learning Outcomes

Assessment opportunity

Exploring reasons why the British Empire expanded; developing relationships between reasons.

Pupils will be able to

- plot trade routes on a map and use these to describe the links between trade and the Empire
- create a table to analyse the change in causes of colonisation post 1870
- create a flow chart to show links between causes of the growth of the empire.

Starter

Worksheet 3.1a(i): this is a very naive quote. More able pupils should question if there was a choice to buy in different parts of the globe and if 'refinement' and 'comfort' was the result of colonial trade globally.

Development

- **Green task:** Using **Worksheets 3.1a(i)** and **(ii)**, pupils plot the route, destination, cost and payment of empire trade as given in **source a**. They should use the map to explain how the growth of trade was linked to the growth of the empire. The more trade increased, the more raw materials and markets were needed, so the empire needed to expand causing an increase in demand, and so on.
- **Blue task:** Pupils tabulate the change in causes of colonisation post 1870: the birth of imperialism fuelled by foreign competition. This highlights how causation changes over time and with different circumstances.
- **Orange task:** As pupils create their flow charts, make links between other causes of colonisation identified earlier. Most causes will link back to imperialistic tendencies even before 1870. This could lead to a discussion of the importance of being the 'workshop of the world' to Britain's heritage. A link could be made to the motivations behind the Great Exhibition 1851 to show world economic dominance even though that was 20 years earlier. Was this the real reason all along? This introduces the concept of informal and formal imperialism. **Worksheet 3.1a(iii)** supports this task.

Plenary

3-2-1: in pairs, pupils to come up with 3 things they have found out, 2 things they would like to know more about, and 1 question they have about what they have learnt.

ICT opportunities

Task 3: the flow chart can be created using ICT. *History in Progress – LiveText CD 2:* electronic activity

3.1 What were the real reasons Britain wanted an empire?

Worksheet 3.1a(i) Building the empire

What else do you need to know?

What can you suggest/infer?

What can you see?

'It is a proud feeling to an Englishman to know that the products of the thousand busy hands and whirling wheels around him are destined to increase the comfort, refinements, or splendour of nations spread far and wide over the globe.' (1839)

3.1 What were the real reasons Britain wanted an empire?

Worksheet 3.1a(ii) Building the empire

Read **source a** below (and on page 134 of *History in Progress – Book 2*).

---

a

The silk of India is woven in Coventry and sold wholesale in New York. It is then shipped to New Orleans where it is sold to a planter. That American planter grows cotton which is exported and woven into cloth in Manchester. This cloth is sold in Bengal in India by a trader. The trader may be paid in part in produce (tea, spices). This produce is sold in the English market 10,000 miles away.

W Felkin, *The Exhibition of 1851*

Now use the information from the source to plot the route, destination, cost and payment of empire trade on the map below. Once you have done that, use the map to explain how the growth of trade was linked to the growth of the empire.

N

3.1 What were the real reasons Britain wanted an empire?

Worksheet 3.1a(iii) Building the empire

1 Carefully read **source d** on page 135 of *History in Progress – Book 2*. Break it down so that you can copy and complete the flow chart below showing what motivated the British to build an empire.

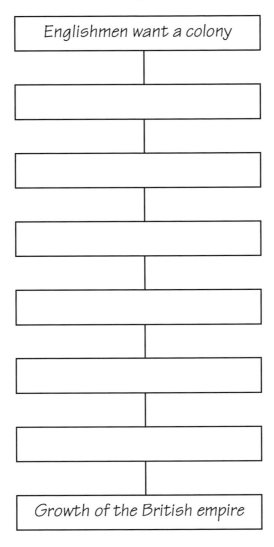

Englishmen want a colony

Growth of the British empire

a) Where on the diagram would you put the other motivations of the British to expand their empire?

- They needed a source of raw materials.
- They needed a market for finished goods.
- Imperialism, the desire to be most powerful in the world.
- Duty to protect natives of the colonies.

b) Discuss your answers with the group. Are your flow charts similar or different? How are they different?

3.2 What was slavery?

3.2a 'A fine business': slavery as a business venture

Learning objectives
- To identify reasons for the Atlantic slave trade.
- To make deductions about human and economic costs of the Atlantic slave trade.

Historical background
That slavery is an old business is easily forgotten when the abolition of slavery in the British Empire has so recently been commemorated. Between 1600 and 1800, it was an immensely profitable business. The discovery of the New World brought new and exotic goods to Europe that acted as a stimulant to both people and trade. This lesson looks at slavery as a business rather than a trade in human misery.

Teaching Activities and Learning Outcomes

Assessment opportunity

Selecting relevant information; sorting and classifying information in order to justify a point of view.

Pupils will be able to

- recognise that people engaged in the slave trade for profit
- interpret data to establish a point of view
- make links between individual sources in order to develop conclusions.

Starter

Pupils answer the starter question on page 136 of *History in Progress – Book 2*. Their responses may be emotionally based, but the debrief should spur them to raise other questions about what sort of society would allow slavery, and the values it has. Responses should be recorded and returned to later.

Development

Green task: The mathematical exercise will help pupils to understand the level of profit they might make in the 'triangle of trade'. Pupils can look at the figures in different ways. For ships' owners, the fitting out of the ship was a huge financial risk, but pupils should also consider the goods taken on board in Britain and how they reflected the priorities of the sailors, as well as when profit was made.

Blue task: Ranking the sources on page 137 encourages pupils to engage with the 'why?' aspect of the Atlantic slave trade. Sharing and attempting to come to a single conclusion promotes discussion which deepens awareness of slavery as a business. **Worksheet 3.2a** provides additional information and, using the 5Ws rule, provides a simple way to eliminate distracting factors.

Orange task: Returning to starter answers and the values identified is useful to divorce modern emotions in order to produce a more objective answer. Asking pupils what characteristics they might expect in such a letter before they start will allow for an element of peer-assessment.

Plenary

Stepping stones: Pupils write key words from the lesson on pieces of paper. Place them on the ground randomly as stepping-stones and ask one pupil to identify the first 'stone'. The class decides which stone is next and why. The exercise both identifies key words and consolidates the links between the words.

Cross-curricular links

Citizenship: Human rights.

ICT opportunities

'Real' costs can be calculated by using a website found on www.heinemann.co.uk/hotlinks.

History in Progress – LiveText CD 2: electronic activity

3.2 What was slavery?

Worksheet 3.2a 'A fine business': slavery as a business venture

Use the following evidence cards to come up with some ideas as to why the trade began in the first place by grouping the information.

Q. Can you suggest titles for the groups that you have come up with?

List your three main reasons why you think the slave trade began and compare these reasons with others in your class.

Q. Is it possible to reduce your list to a single reason and how would you justify it?

Sao Tomé	Slaves transported		Liverpool
This island colony was established in 1493 off the African coast. By the mid-1500s the Portuguese settlers, using slave labour, had turned the islands into Africa's foremost exporter of sugar.	Portugal	4.6 million	Merchants developed expert knowledge of the trade and established good contacts with traders on the African coast. They knew which goods to send to Africa and which would sell on different parts of the coast.
	Spain	1.6 million	
	France	1.25 million	
	Holland	0.5 million	
	Britain	2.6 million	

The English	Productivity	A modern view
… brandies, tobacco, sugar; deals and timber for building; oil, wine, spice, raw silks, calico, chocolate, coffee, tea; on some of these the taxes are more than doubled. And yet they have their parlours set off with the tea-table and the chocolate-pot. **Daniel Defoe**	If you go to Barbados, you shall see a flourishing island, with many able men. I believe that they have brought this year no less than 1,000 negroes and in a year and a half, they will earn as much as they cost. **Rev. George Downing, Chaplin of a merchant ship 1645**	Taken together, the new drugs gave English society an almighty hit; the Empire, it might be said, was built on a huge sugar, caffeine, and nicotine rush – a rush nearly everyone could experience. **Niall Ferguson, *Empire***

Number of slave trading voyages by country		Barbados	Plantations
Portugal	30000	Once established on the Caribbean island, sugar production increased rapidly, with Barbados experiencing an increase from 7,000 to 12,000 tons produced per year between 1655 and 1700.	Sao Tomé provided the blueprint for the larger plantation economy of the Americas.
Spain	4000		
France	4200		
Holland	2000		
Britain	12000		

Cargo list for a ship going to Africa from Bristol

An estimate for a cargo to buy 250 Negroes in Nigeria:
80 rolls of blue chintz cloth
100 rolls of cotton cloth with fine small stripes (small)
100 rolls of cotton cloth with fine small stripes (large)
100 cotton rolls with red and blue mixed stripe.

British sugar imports

Sugar
Weight in thousand pounds

Year	Weight
1700	668
1750	1270
1800	4301
1850	9787

Where slaves were sold to

Brazil	4.0 m
Spanish Empire	2.5 m
British West Indies	2.0 m
French West Indies	1.6 m
British North America	0.5 m
Europe	0.2 m

Numbers of slaves working in different areas

Sugar plantations	5m
Coffee plantations	2m
Mines	1m
Domestic labour	2m
Cotton fields	0.5m
Cocoa fields	0.25m
Building	0.25m

The price of a slave in South Carolina

1724	£22.09
1752	£36.91
1755	£41.4
1771	£49.74
1784	£67.82
1806	£70.66

British tobacco imports

Year	Weight in thousand pounds
1700	315
1750	481
1800	357
1850	355

The value of slaves

The average price of a prime field hand in Georgia in 1860 was US$1,800.

Prices in South Carolina in 1859 ranged from US$1,000 for a girl aged 12 to 15, to US$1,500 for a male aged 20 to 26.

British tea imports

Year	Weight in thousand pounds
1700	14
1750	484
1800	1510
1850	5051

The outward voyage

The outward voyage from Bristol was made with trinkets, beads, copper rods, cotton goods, guns and alcohol which were to be traded for slaves off the coast of West Africa.

British coffee imports

Year	Weight in thousand pounds
1700	36
1750	75
1800	3,988
1850	3,172

1790

In 1790 South Carolina contained less than 3% of America's slave population; and it produced rice and indigo, whereas the overwhelming reason slaves were brought across the Atlantic was sugar.

Attitude to slaves

'What is all this talk of human people being thrown overboard? This is a case of goods. It is a case about throwing over of goods. They are goods and property.'

From a speech by a lawyer representing the owners of a slave ship where slaves had been thrown overboard.

3.2 What was slavery?

3.2b Slave conditions

Learning objectives
- To find out about the conditions slaves had to live under.
- To use sources to present information to an audience.

Historical background
For those trapped in the system of slavery, from the moment of capture to the time of their death, life was reduced to a level where finding a way of getting through each day was the main achievement. The shock of capture, the squalor of the voyage across the Atlantic, the degradation of being sold was followed by an often all-too-short life of servitude.

Teaching Activities and Learning Outcomes

Assessment opportunity

Using selected source materials to present a considered view of the conditions suffered by slaves.

Pupils will be able to

- use some sources to be able to describe a simple view of slave conditions
- select sources that explain how slaves were treated
- select and deploy sources to reflect a specific viewpoint on slave conditions.

Starter

The starter task on page 138 of *History in Progress – Book 2* should be completed individually, before allowing pupils to pair and share. The debrief should focus on criteria for the selection. Grouping reasons for the selection of each picture should produce a multitude of answers that can be used to encourage pupils to think about the importance of such a selection in producing materials for a wider audience.

Development

Green task: Pupils should develop open questions that will allow for longer responses. To help them recognise the chronology, pupils could be asked for at least one question for each picture and two further questions that link some of the pictures. Tasks 2 and 3 ask pupils to consider slave conditions from two different viewpoints. In pairs, they study relevant sources for details that support a specific view. Pairs then share their viewpoints with the whole class.

Blue task: This task needs to be treated sensitively with teachers having prior knowledge of any specific bereavement in the group before embarking on the exercise. It can be personalised further by asking pupils to use only selected sources. The introduction of the slave owner into the graveside eulogy poses a 'reality' question for the pupils. A more significant question that could be developed orally that tests a deeper understanding of the situation could be: Why should I change the speech?

Orange task: Pupils have the opportunity to justify a viewpoint using the sources provided and the experiences of the exercises in the early part of the lesson. In order to judge the quality of the presentations, pupils should consider success criteria of good presentations before they start the exercise. **Worksheet 3.2b** gives some guidance on how this might be shared with the group. This method of assessing the work supports the use of peer assessment in the group.

Plenary

Primary source: Select ONE source that you think summarises the key features of slave conditions? Why did you choose this source?

ICT opportunities

History in Progress – LiveText CD 2: electronic activity

3.2 What was slavery?

Worksheet 3.2b(i) Slave conditions

Q. What criteria do you think should go in the empty boxes to provide a grid to help judge the presentations?

Grading criteria	Introduction	Use of sources	Conclusion
• Good	Clear introduction that sets out the purpose of the work		
• Satisfactory	Has an introduction but lacks detail	Uses some sources to support the viewpoints being shared	A conclusion is present with some links back to the question
• Further development	Has no clear introduction to the work		

3.2 What was slavery?

Worksheet 3.2b(ii) Slave Conditions

A typical slave's day from the Annaberg sugar mill, Virgin Islands.

4am	Get up and feed the livestock.
5am	Reporting to work in the field.
8am	Break for rest and breakfast. (Those slaves without food would eat sugarcane, when available.)
12–12.30pm	Grass gathered to feed cattle.
12.30–2pm	Lunch. Slaves with families would go home. Slaves without families generally stayed in the fields during the lunch break.
2pm–sunset	Worked the fields to sunset. During the dead season, July to November, when there were no sugarcane crops, the animals were fed again, and the slaves could return home for the evening meal and the preparation of the next day's lunch.
7–10pm	Additional work called 'donker work'. This was night work, such as hauling manure and water or cleaning up the master's yard.

What was slavery?

3.2c Did slavery transform Britain?

Learning objectives
- To be able to develop an historical opinion using source material.
- To explain why slavery changed the city of Liverpool.

Historical background
With a modern perspective it is difficult to understand that for the best part of 200 years the slave trade was considered just another business. Cities like Glasgow, Bristol and especially Liverpool grew rich on the profits to be made from the trade, as the fine buildings from this period in those towns lay testament. The business of slavery was consequently a driver behind changes occurring in Britain at the time.

Teaching Activities and Learning Outcomes

Assessment opportunity

Using source material to produce judgements that identify the nature and importance of change.

Pupils will be able to

- use a source document to identify features of change in a city
- select sources to identify key changes in a city
- evaluate the impact of slavery on the development of a city.

Starter

Pupils answer the starter question on page 142 of *History in Progress – Book 2*. An example of a nearby expanding town could be given, allowing pupils to develop their lists. Pupils can also prioritise answers as a group to identify key factors that might be present in the towns in the rest of the lesson.

Development

Green task: This task can use the factors for town development from the starter. For differentiation, attention can be drawn to specific aspects that relate to developing wealth in Bristol. Debriefing this exercise can focus on how the wealth being generated in the city affected its growth.

Blue task: The word limit focuses attention on key issues. Pupils can only choose three sources from page 143. In debriefing, pupils identify changes and how their choice of sources shows this. Redoing the exercise with specific sources and comparing the results against the pupils' original work provides an extension.

Orange task: In order to personalise this task specific sources could be identified. Pupils could use a spider diagram to identify changes that affected an individual who lived through this time before writing begins. An extension could focus on whether things had changed for the better and what criteria pupils used to make that judgement.

Plenary

How many factors identified at the start of the lesson explain the development of cities like Bristol and Liverpool, and what other factors are not true of today's expanding towns?

Cross-curricular links

Geography: The human processes that cause change and development.

ICT opportunities

An electronic whiteboard version of the image could be used for the task 1 using the Livetext resource bank. The spotlight tool can draw pupils' attention to aspects of the image.

History in Progress – LiveText CD 2: electronic activity

3.2 What was slavery?

3.2d Abolition

Learning objectives
- To learn about what different people valued at the turn of the nineteenth century.
- To be able distinguish between the types and nature of the arguments that were being made

Historical background
In the 200 years since the abolition of slavery in the British Empire, few have questioned that it was the right thing to do. But in the last quarter of the eighteenth century there was considerable disquiet about outlawing a business that was legal and profitable. It took patience, guile and in the end skilful politicians to achieve abolition and William Wilberforce is one name which stands out among the abolitionists.

Teaching Activities and Learning Outcomes

Assessment opportunity

Evaluating, within a historical context, the strength and depth of opposing viewpoints.

Pupils will be able to

- recognise key points in the struggle against slavery
- use sources to develop a broad argument either for or against slavery
- evaluate the arguments for or against slavery through the use of select sources.

Starter

Pupils read the poem then answer the questions on page 144 of *History in Progress – Book 2*. Given their prior knowledge, is it an accurate representation of slave conditions? Examining the purpose of the poem should raise questions about the poet, and where the poem was published and why.

Development

Green task: The hook in the task is to identify a point in Wilberforce's career that was a turning point. Pupils will need to be made aware that turning points are not necessarily the end of the struggle. The exercise might ask for individual points of view in the debrief before asking for a group decision. This will allow discussion as to the criteria used to make the decision.

Blue task: The use of a spider diagram helps pupils to organise opinions from the sources more clearly, although some might prefer to use a list. Asking them to prioritise the arguments gives a chance for the group to challenge each other on what they believe are the key issues and why. The depth of feeling in this debate can be exaggerated by the use of a final class vote to provide a single answer.

Orange task: Using groups of six is designed to stimulate debate and highlight opinions they have come across. The observer's role is not only to listen to the arguments, but also to clarify the positions of those taking part through questions. They then need to feedback their findings and thoughts to the rest of the group. Asking for conclusions based on what they have heard can extend this exercise.

Plenary

Pupils could use prior knowledge to construct a brief poem putting the slaver's side of the argument or alternatively about the importance of Wilberforce and his fellow colleagues in delivering abolition.

Cross-curricular links

English: Starter and plenary exercises support literacy, asking pupils to write imaginatively and correctly.

ICT opportunities

History in Progress – LiveText CD 2: electronic activity

3.2 What was slavery?

3.2e Taking it further!: How has slavery been interpreted?

Learning objectives
- To be able to understand how slavery can been interpreted in differing ways.
- To use source evidence to explain how differing historical interpretations are developed.

Historical background
'Slavery was a bad thing.' This statement depends on many different factors, not least the evidence used to make such a bold claim. The huge amount of material available would seem to support the view, but a historian should be sceptical. Therefore, looking for evidence as to the benefits of slavery is essential to a balanced viewpoint. Determining the quality of the material on which judgements are made is also vital.

Teaching Activities and Learning Outcomes

Assessment opportunity
Critically using source material to develop historical interpretation skills

Pupils will be able to
- identify historical interpretations from differing viewpoints
- explain how the type of source selected can influence the nature of historical interpretation
- select sources to produce a specific historical interpretation.

Starter
The initial question on page 148 of *History in Progress – Book 2* asks pupils to give opinions. A follow-up question would be to ask what source material would provide evidence to back up their opinion.

Development
The ability to interpret diverse source material is at the core of the questions set in this lesson. First, pupils use the Nature/Origin/Purpose technique to look at the sources. As a precursor to the exercise, the pupils could look at an unrelated artefact to establish the concept of NOP. To debrief the task, focus on differences in answers and whether the interpretation matters when making historical judgements. The same questions could be posed when looking at the two sources provided, with a tight focus on whether how we understand slavery as historians is determined by the type of sources available to us.

Additional sources then help develop the pupil's understanding of the concepts. Sharing answers raises questions of validity and value. A 'devil's advocate' response that neither is useful adds further challenge.

The spider diagram consolidates the concept by asking pupils to look back across the slavery sections. This should be developed in such a way that pupils are able to clearly see the different NOPs ahead of the final exercise. To extend the activity, pupils can rate which aspect they felt was the most important or prioritise the sources on one aspect of NOP to understand whether they have greater or lesser value.

The final question asks pupils to use selected sources in a specific context. This could be answered in many ways (written, debate, presentation) but the focus should be on seeking to answer the contextual question. Pupils can then consider whether the evidence we use to make judgements can be trusted.

Plenary
High 5: What five things should we remember about the slave trade? To debrief, highlight the features that are most important to pupils. It can be followed by asking for one aspect they want to know more about.

Cross-curricular links
English: Develop reflective, critical and discriminating responses to a wide range of texts.

ICT opportunities
History in Progress – LiveText CD 2: electronic activity

Unit 3 Moving and travelling

Assessment Unit 3

3.3 Assessment task 1: What were the arguments for and against slavery?

Pupils will be able to

- recognise that sources can be interpreted differently
- use evidence to produce opposing view points
- evaluate evidence to reach a conclusion based on opposing sources.

What the task is about

- The task requires pupils to work through a series of smaller questions before producing an 'upside down booklet' that asks them to use selected historical evidence to deliver polarised historical interpretations of the slave trade.

- The first questions encourage pupils to question the nature of a source and what it is trying to convey. The picture extract is deliberately not an image that pupils would expect to see in relation to slavery, and they should be encouraged to discuss the purpose of the painting and the artistic devices used within it to portray its messages. They could use **Worksheet 3.3a(i)** to help them.

- Attention should be drawn to the power of the title of a painting, and how titles can be used to convey additional meaning to an otherwise lifeless work.

- The third question challenges the student to consider the utility of this and other sources in creating or understanding a historical interpretation. Clearly there is no correct answer, but pupils could be encouraged to reflect on situations when they would use / not use a source.

- The booklet itself asks student to write two one sided views of the slave trade. The booklet is evenly split, and care should be taken to insist that if images/quotes are included, that they are the same number and size in both sections. The challenge here is to balance the extreme views rather than to produce work something bland in the middle. They could use **Worksheet 3.3a(ii)** to help them.

- ICT could be used to produce a template for the activity that works better in a written form than in electronic.

- A markscheme for this task is provided on **Worksheet 3.3b.**

Unit 3 Assessment 1

Worksheet 3.3a(i)

What were the arguments for and against slavery?

Look at the picture below. On one side of the image highlight any benefits that slavery brought to the people in the picture. On the other side highlight anything negative that you think slavery brought to people in the picture.

What title might you give to this image? Write down three different titles and compare them with a classmate.

Title 1: _____.

Title 2: _____.

Title 3: _____.

Between the two of you choose just one title and explain why you chose it.

Unit 3 Assessment 1

Worksheet 3.3a(ii)

What were the arguments for and against slavery?

Before starting on the 'upside down' booklet, you need to ask some questions about the evidence you are going to use. Look again at this image. Some questions have been suggested for you, but what other questions would you like to ask before you start to use it or similar images in your assessment?

- Who painted this?

- When was it painted?

- Why was it painted?

- Did this really happen?

- What is it trying to show?

- Should I include this?

- Should I leave this out?

- Other questions:

Unit 3 Assessment 1

Worksheet 3.3b

How did you do?

Level 4: I was able to ...	
describe some of the features and events of the slave trade and shown that there were changes throughout the period.	
use evidence to show that the slave trade can be interpreted in different ways.	
begin to structure my information to put forward simple arguments for and against slavery.	
describe some of the features and events of the slave trade and show that there were changes throughout the period.	

Level 5: I was able to ...	
describe some of the features and events of the slave trade to show that these affected different people in different ways.	
begin to suggest reasons why the evidence can provide differing interpretations for the slave trade.	
begin to carefully select your information to make structured arguments for and against slavery.	
describe some of the features and events of the slave trade to show that these affected different people in different ways.	

Level 6: I was able to ...	
begin to explain why some of the features and events of the slave trade affected different people in different ways.	
begin to explain how and why the evidence can provide differing interpretations for the slave trade.	
carefully focus my information to produce strong and convincing arguments for and against slavery.	
begin to explain why some of the features and events of the slave trade affected different people in different ways.	

Things I did well: _____

I need to learn more about: _____

One thing I need to improve is: _____

I will do this by: _____

Teacher comment: _____

_____

Pupil comment: _____

_____

3.4 Why did people go exploring?

3.4a Cook's voyages of discovery

Learning objectives
- To investigate the voyages made by Captain Cook.
- To make a judgment about the significance Cook's voyages.

Historical background
Maritime exploration was still of great importance to European powers in the nineteenth century, keen to compete for prestige, increase the size of their empires and develop riches through trade with new lands. Cook's expedition of the 1760s to the Southern Hemisphere was given to him under secret orders. Dutch explorers had already discovered much of the western coast of 'Australia', but it was still believed that Australia made up most of the Southern Hemisphere. Cook showed this to be untrue when he discovered the eastern coast of Australia. He made extremely accurate maps of Australia, New Zealand and several Pacific Islands. Cook's voyages also provided information about new kinds of wildlife (e.g. the kangaroo), birds and flowers which were important for science. Additionally, he established relations with the native peoples of New Zealand (Maori) and Australia (Aborigines).

Teaching Activities and Learning Outcomes

Homework

Pupils research the voyage/journey of another nineteenth-century explorer that changed people's knowledge and understanding of the world, e.g. Charles Darwin, David Livingstone.

Pupils will be able to

- identify the top five discoveries that Cook made
- write key notes for a speech about the importance of Cook's voyages
- write a newspaper article outlining the importance of Cook's discoveries.

Starter

Pupils answer the questions about the map on page 152 in *History in Progress – Book 2*. Reasons for inaccuracies: the lack of voyages of exploration; inaccuracies in measuring and charting tools; no satellites or aerial photographs available.

Development

Green task: Pupils work with a partner to select their top five discoveries. They could then join with another pair before eventually taking whole class feedback to compile the class top five.

Blue task: Pupils select key points for inclusion in a speech about the importance of Cook at the unveiling of a statue of him. This task is best preceded by discussion about the types of significance as this will encourage pupils to justify their selections.

Orange task: Pupils have the opportunity to summarise what they have learned about the significance of Cook's voyage by writing an article. They should be encouraged to organise their article into sections and clearly express their judgement about the significance of his voyage.

Plenary

3-2-1: Pupils to note down three things they have learned in this lesson, two ways in which they learned and one thing they would like to find out more about.

ICT opportunities

History in Progress – LiveText CD 2: electronic activity

3.4 Why did people go exploring?

3.4b An Arctic mystery

Learning objectives

- Discover what happened to the explorers who went missing in the Arctic in 1845.
- Evaluate the reliability of the evidence to make a judgment about what really happened to the explorers.

Historical background

Maritime exploration was still the source of much competition between the European powers into the nineteenth century for reasons of prestige, empire building and trade. One remaining challenge was to discover a north-west passage through the Arctic seas. Franklin's 1845 expedition of two ships set out to do this, but they never returned. The north-west passage was only successfully negotiated by ship by the Norwegian explorer Amunsen at the start of the twentieth century. Nowadays, ice-breaker ships make it much easier to sail through the Arctic; prior to these ships many of the channels were impassable.

Teaching Activities and Learning Outcomes

Assessment opportunity

Explaining the causes of events.

Pupils will be able to

- identify and make links between reasons why the explorers went missing from the map
- evaluate the reliability of evidence about the fate of the explorers
- draw conclusions about what happened to the explorers which makes links between the causes.

Starter

Gimme 5: Pupils suggest five reasons why people might explore the Arctic today, e.g. for adventure, prestige, environmental and nature research. Ask pupils to think how these reasons might differ from those in the nineteenth century when the concern was more to find a passage through the ice (the north-west passage) to facilitate quicker access around the world by ship.

Development

Green task: Pupils select evidence from the map on page 154 of *History in Progress – Book 2* to help them explain why explorers disappeared. They should start connect these reasons. It might be helpful for pupils to record their ideas on a spider diagram so they can draw in the links.

Blue task: Pupils should be encouraged to identify aspects of Dickens' account which are only based on his opinion and are not backed up by factual evidence from the expedition, and aspects that show Dickens' prejudice against the evidence given by the Eskimos for no good reasons, all of which lessens the reliability of his account.

Orange task: As in task 1, encourage pupils to make links between factors. For example, after explorers became trapped in ice, the lead poisoning in their food weakened them, made them irritable and less likely to cooperate with each other in the search for food and escape so as their food supplies ran out they were unable to improve their situation. As more men died the survivors, increasingly short of food, may have resorted to cannibalism in a desperate attempt to stay alive. Ultimately all failed.

Plenary

In pairs pupils suggest places left to explore today, e.g. space, the ocean, rainforests, etc.

ICT opportunities

History in Progress – LiveText CD 2: electronic activity

3.5 Who had to leave?

3.5a Escaping the Irish Famine

Learning objectives
- To discover information about the Great Famine in Ireland in the 1840s.
- To explore the different reasons why people emigrated to other countries.

Historical background
In 1845 the worst tragedy to hit Ireland occurred: the Irish potato famine. It left many families unemployed, homeless and starving. Despite the British government's attempts to help the struggling Irish population, many of them emigrated to England or America. However, some ship captains took advantage of the desperation felt by the Irish and cheated them out of a full passage abroad.

Teaching Activities and Learning Outcomes

Assessment opportunity
Making links between the reasons why people chose to emigrate as a result of the Irish potato famine.

Pupils will be able to
- sort reasons for emigrating into 'push' and 'pull' factors
- create a prioritised list of reasons for emigrating and explain their ordering
- write a letter explaining why someone might have emigrated from Ireland in the 1840s.

Starter
Think, pair, share: Pupils discuss how help is provided to people caught up in a natural disaster. Ask them to think about the flooding in Bangladesh in 2007, Hurricane *Katrina* in New Orleans in 2006 or the 2004 Boxing Day tsunami. What effects did these disasters have on their local population? What relief aid was sent from other countries? Once pupils have shared their ideas, make the link between this and the Irish potato famine, and the lack of support received from Britain. Pupils can then look at **sources a** and **b** on p156 of *History in Progress – Book 2*.

Development
Green task: Give pupils a copy of **Worksheet 3.5a**. Working in groups they should examine the cards explaining why people would move from Ireland, and sort them into 'push' and 'pull' factors. Each member of the group should be able to explain why they have made the decision they have.

Blue task: Pupils rank the 'push' and 'pull' cards in the order of priority with the most important reason first and the least important reason last. Pupils should make a note of their lists along with an explanation of why they have selected the most and least important 'push' and 'pull' factors.

Orange task: Pupils place themselves in the position of an Irish immigrant who has survived the journey to a new country and is writing a letter home. In the letter, pupils must include information about why they left Ireland, their journey and what life is like in their new country. Remind pupils to follow standard letter conventions.

Plenary
Picture this!: In pairs or small groups, pupils take turns to draw a key word or theme from the lesson while the other pupils guess what it is.

ICT opportunities
For websites with more information about Irish migration, go to www.heinemann.co.uk/hotlinks.

History in Progress – LiveText CD 2: electronic activity

3.5 Who had to leave?

Worksheet 3.5a: Why did people leave Ireland?

1   In pairs, read the ten cards on this page, which give reasons why people might move to another country. Then arrange them into 'push' and 'pull' factors. Explain to another pair or group how you came to your decision.

2 a) In the pair you started with in task 1, put your 'push' cards in order of what you think is the most important reason people left Ireland (the least important reason should be on the bottom). Now do the same with your 'pull' cards.

  b) Make a note of your lists, explaining why you chose the most important and least important 'push' and 'pull' factors.

Card 1: Community

There were large communities of Irish people living in big cities in North America including Toronto and Ontario in Canada, and Boston and New York. They provided food and money for Irish people arriving in their cities.

Card 2: Youth

Young people in particular could find work in America and could send money back to Ireland to help their relatives.

Card 3: Potatoes

More than one-third of Irish people ate nothing but potatoes. From 1845 to 1849 the potato crop was destroyed by a fungus. Between 1845 and 1851 between 1.1 million and 1.5 million Irish people died from the effects of the famine.

Card 4: Land

Most of the land in Ireland was owned by a small number of people. The large majority of Irish people had little chance of owning more than a tiny plot of land.

Card 5: Work

Lancashire and Yorkshire in England were attractive places to move to because there was plenty of work in the factories and fields.

Card 6: Transport

Transport on ships (known as 'coffin ships') to America was very cheap. Getting to England was also cheap. In the 1840s it cost just 1/2 a penny to travel from Cork to London.

Card 7: Government

In 1846 the British government tried to help the starving people in Ireland by providing work such as mending roads through public work schemes. In February 1847 the government encouraged the setting up around 600 soup kitchens but in late 1847 these soup kitchens were closed.

Card 8: Landlords

Some landlords were kind to their starving tenants giving them food and not making them pay their rents. Other landlords were not so kind, throwing their tenants out of their houses in what is known as 'eviction'.

Card 9: Railways

Railways were being built across Britain and America in the 1840s. There was plenty of work for railways labourers, who became known as 'navvies'.

Card 10: Food supply

The British government imported grain from Canada to help the starving. But, rather than giving the grain away, the government sold it.

© Pearson Education Ltd 2008: *History in Progress – Planning and Resource Pack 2*

3.5 Who had to leave?

3.5b The Highland Clearances

Learning objectives
- To learn about the events of the Highland Clearances in Scotland during the eighteenth century.
- To develop the ability to explain in detail a single point of view backed up with evidence.

Historical background
During the nineteenth century the Scottish Highlands were home to the Scottish Clans. Ruled by clan chieftains they had made a living there for generations and life had stayed the same for years. But this changed in 1745 after the Scottish lost to the English army at the Battle of Culloden. The Clan Chieftains became interested in making money and pleasing their new English landlords, which eventually led to the Highland Clearances.

Teaching Activities and Learning Outcomes

Assessment opportunity

Writing a speech from a clan chief to his clan explaining why he is working with the English landlords to clear the Highlands.

Pupils will be able to

- write an explanation from the point of view of a clan chieftain
- write two paragraphs about the Clearances each from a different point of view
- identify similarities and differences between the ways in which the Scottish and Irish were treated.

Starter

Explain to pupils what a clan is, then ask them to try to suggest a modern-day equivalent, e.g. a religious or political group or even a sports affiliation. They can then look at the picture on p158 of *History in Progress – Book 2*.

Development

Green task: Pupils imagine they are a clan chieftain and write an explanation to their family about why they have made the decision to work for the English instead of supporting their clan. Less able students should be encouraged to give at least two reasons; more able should write more. For task 1b pupils re-examine the explanation they have written but from the point of view of a modern historian.

Blue task: This task is designed to help pupils develop their empathy skills. They are required to think about the Clearances from two differing points of view. Less able pupils could be encouraged to work in pairs, with each one of the pair taking a different point of view.

Orange task: Pupils work with a partner to make a list of the differences between how the Scottish were treated compared with the Irish during their times of difficulties.

Plenary

Decision time: Decide in their pairs whether they think the Irish or the Scottish were treated worse by the British in the nineteenth century. Remind pupils to give a reason for their decision.

ICT opportunities

History in Progress – LiveText CD 2: electronic activity

3.5 Who had to leave?

3.5c Taking it further!: Remembering the Highland Clearances

Learning objectives

- To understand and explore different interpretations of the Duke of Sutherland and how these have arisen.

Historical background

The Highland Clearances that occurred after the Battle of Culloden in 1745 was one of the worst tragedies to happen in the history of Scotland. Many Scottish families still look back at the Highland Clearances and feel angry at the way their families were treated. In an effort to make sure that the thousands of deaths during the clearances are not forgotten, monuments and plaques have been erected. Some of these monuments have caused great controversy.

Teaching Activities and Learning Outcomes

Assessment opportunity

Exploring differing interpretations and the reasons behind these; coming up with their own interpretation based on primary sources.

Pupils will be able to

- form opinions about the type of person the Duke of Sutherland was
- write a letter arguing either for or against plans to erect a different monument
- design a more appropriate monument.

Starter

Ask pupils to examine **source a** (a photograph of a statue of the Duke of Sutherland) on page 160 of *History in Progress – Book 2*. Give pupils up to 2 minutes to suggest, in pairs, why the statue was built.

Development

- The tasks are all linked and designed to make pupils think about why monuments are built and how the impact of history can still be felt today.
- **Task 1** asks pupils why monuments have been built for the Highland Clearances, while **task 2** asks why they feel the Duke of Sutherland was chosen to go on top of the monument. Make links back to the starter activity here.
- **Task 3** requires pupils to explain what impression they now have of the Duke of Sutherland and then reflect on whether their answers were correct from task 2.
- In **tasks 4a** and **4b** pupils need to decide whether a more appropriate and reflective monument is needed by the residents of Golspie in Scotland, which they will then design as part of **task 5**.

Plenary

Each pupil should provide one new fact they have learned in the lesson without repeating another person's fact.

ICT opportunities

Students can use the Internet to research appropriate monuments, then use Word or PowerPoint to design their monument for homework.

History in Progress – LiveText CD 2: electronic activity

3.6 What was the impact of steam on transport?

3.6a Life at sea

Learning objectives
- To find out about the advantages and disadvantages of sailing ships.
- To find out what life was like on board a sailing ship.

Historical background
Britain's wealth, power and prestige in the eighteenth and nineteenth centuries in many ways relied on its control of the seas. In the eighteenth century the main ships used for trade between Britain and the Far East were the East Indiamen sailing ships. These were fast ships crewed by over 100 men which could carry large and profitable cargoes of tea, silks and spices. However, by the nineteenth century it was increasingly recognised that there were limitations with sailing ships, which were to be replaced by the end of that century with steam ships.

Teaching Activities and Learning Outcomes

Assessment opportunity
Evaluating the advantages and disadvantages of sailing ships as trading ships in the eighteenth and nineteenth centuries.

Pupils will be able to
- identify the top three criticisms of sailing ships that a sailor might have had.
- identify the main problems connected to wind power
- write a letter persuading a trading company to buy steam powered ships.

Starter
Pupils look at **source a** on page 162 and, in pairs, suggest at least two ways in which naval power was so important to Britain in the nineteenth century. Suggestions might include the importance of ships in trade, prosperity, defence and maintaining an empire.

Development
Green task: Pupils identify the advantages and disadvantages of relying on sailing ships to carry trade between India and Britain. This task also offers opportunity for empathy with pupils thinking about the criticisms from the point of view of a nineteenth century sailor.

Blue task: This task focuses on one of the major disadvantages: reliance on wind power. Then it broadens this out by asking pupils to suggest other disadvantages.

Orange task: Pupils write a persuasive letter. Encourage them to organise and structure their explanation around issues such as profitability, reliability, length of journey and comfort of the voyage. They should also give examples to support their main points.

Plenary
Lead a 5-minute discussion in which pairs are asked to anticipate the ways in which steam ships might overcome some of the limitations of sailing ships which they have highlighted. Do they think that steam ships will be better in all ways to sailing ships? This discussion will anticipate the **Lesson 3.3b**, which focuses on the advantages of steam ships.

ICT opportunities
History in Progress – LiveText CD 2: electronic activity

3.6 What was the impact of steam on transport?

3.6b Steam versus sail

Learning objectives
- To understand the advantages of the invention of steam ships.
- To identify the impact of steam ships in the nineteenth century.

Historical background
The invention of steam power from the 1760s transformed transport possibilities through the steam train and the steam-powered boat. Steam ships were not so dependent on tides, winds or currents as sail ships, which opened up new commercial possibilities for ships. Soon tourist steamer services were operating and perishable goods could be transported with greater reliability. However, the age of the sailing ship was not over. Sail was still the preferred method of transporting tea from India and China, as the clipper ships of the mid-nineteenth century benefited from large cargo space and could travel very quickly with good winds. However, developments in the steam engine continued to make it faster, more economical and more reliable, so that by the end of the century steam had almost entirely replaced sail.

Teaching Activities and Learning Outcomes

Assessment opportunity

Judging the significance of the invention of steam steams to water transport.

Pupils will be able to

- design a poster advertising the advantages of steam ships and suggest arguments against them
- make decisions about the advantages of different types of ship
- draw conclusions about how significant a change was brought about in water transport by the invention of the steam ship.

Starter

Using **source a** on page 164 of *History in Progress – Book 2* ask pupils to draw conclusions about steam and sailing ships from it. The painting suggests the steam tug is pulling the sailing ship along, which means the end of sail power. Some pupils might notice that Turner seems to think the end of sailing power sad. The *Temeraire* was one of the most important ships alongside the *Victory* at the Battle of Trafalgar in 1805.

Development

Green task: Pupils identify the advantages of steam ships by designing an advertisement for a new steam boat passenger service. They should be encouraged to use examples to support their points.

Blue task: Pupils make decisions about the most appropriate mode of ship to use based on the type of journey they wish to complete. **Worksheet 3.6b** supports this task. Part b could be a discussion.

Orange task: Pupils make a judgement about how significant a change was brought about in water transport by the invention of steam ships: a turning point, no change, a significant change whose full effects were felt later. This task would be best preceded by discussion in order to encourage pupils to sully justify their ideas with examples.

Plenary

Vote with your feet: Pupils show which of the statements in task 4 they agree with most by moving to allocated parts of the classroom. They should be prepared to explain their decision.

ICT opportunities

History in Progress – LiveText CD 2: electronic activity

3.6 What was the impact of steam on transport?

Worksheet 3.6b Steam ships

Complete the table to show which type of ship you would choose for each journey in 1850, before the Suez Canal was built.

Journey	Type of ship (sail or steam)	Reason for choice
1 A tourist passenger boat service on the River Clyde in Scotland.		
2 To transport tea from China.		
3 To transport milk from Holland.		
4 To transport wool from Australia.		
5 A passenger service between Britain and America.		

Which of the answers to this question would you change if you were completing the table in 1869 after the Suez Canal was built? Why?

_____

_____

_____

_____

3.6 What was the impact of steam on transport?

3.6c Why the railways?

Learning objectives
- To identify reasons for the development of an alternative form of transport in the nineteenth century.
- To be able to assess the nature of change that happened to Victorian business because of the growth of the railways.

Historical background
Railways were nothing new in the early nineteenth century. There had been examples of goods being carried on tracks in Europe for many years. The difference was the connection of the steam engine with tracked transport. The viability of developing a locomotive had been doubted for all sorts of reasons, from the sheer weight of such a machine, to the presence of alternatives; such as stationary engines hauling chains to which goods wagons were attached. However, it was the locomotive engine that was to prevail.

Teaching Activities and Learning Outcomes

Assessment opportunity

Constructing a persuasive argument using the key factors behind the success of the railways.

Pupils will be able to

- recognise the problems of road and canal transport
- give reasons as to why the railway was an improvement over existing forms of transport
- produce a convincing argument for the development of the railway.

Starter

Pupils consider the changes to everyday life by the invention of a radical, alternative form of transport. Ask them for the effect it would have on their own lives or the things that would no longer be needed. The focus for pupils needs to be on what changes to ordinary life people could expect to happen, and whether there is a possibility of further change in the future.

Development

Green task: Pupils consider possible push factors – things that encouraged people of the time to want to have alternative forms of transport. Gathering the ideas together there is an opportunity to identify, without going into detail, the characteristics of an alternative form of transport. This could be referred back to at the end of the lesson.

Blue task: This task could be treated as a hot seat *Dragon's Den* exercise with pupils asked to consider additional questions that they would like to ask the person wanting investment. The debrief should focus on whether, given the risk of a railway and the quality of the answers, the investment should go ahead and why.

Orange task: This task focuses on the impact of the railway, and the advantages that it had for businesses at the time.

Plenary

After the arrival of the railway, canal and road transport continued to operate for many years. What sorts of things would canal and road-using businesses be promoting to stop people moving to the railways?

ICT opportunities

History in Progress – LiveText CD 2: electronic activity

3.6 What was the impact of steam on transport?

3.6d Impact of the railways

Learning objectives
- To find out about the ways railway transformed life for ordinary people.
- To judge how significant an impact the coming of the railway had to ordinary people's lives.

Historical background
The opening of the Liverpool to Manchester line in 1830 is often seen as a historical turning point. Although the original purpose of this inter-city line was to improve business, its success led to an expansion of the rail network that was to continue for the next 75 years. The result in Britain was dramatic with changes in business, social and economic life across the nineteenth century.

Teaching Activities and Learning Outcomes

Assessment opportunity

Defining and defending a historical viewpoint based on selected data; sorting and reorganising information to help evaluate.

Pupils will be able to

- describe differing attitudes held towards the railway from source materials
- select relevant information from a text to reach a conclusion
- use criteria to evaluate the impact of the railways.

Starter

Gimme 5: Pupils contribute to a class list of five ways that slower transport might affect their way of life. This can be completed through discussion, the use of a spider diagram or through a list.

Development

Green task: Pupils list adjectives describing the attitudes of the people **sources a–d** on page 168 of *History in Progress – Book 2* towards the railway. This can be done in pairs before feeding back to the rest of the group, or through the individual images being annotated. The focus of the feedback should be on attitudinal change and could be completed by comparing the first and last image to identify differences.

Blue task: The task could be completed as individuals to allow pupils to reach their own conclusions, but an alternative, to work as a trio, encourages small group work. Pupils could also be asked whether the evidence they have been provided with is sufficient to reach a conclusion, and what additional resources they might need.

Orange task: Looking at the criteria behind their choices, when sorting, could debrief the first exercise. For the final aspect of the task, pupils can include further areas within their original order, or make a judgement by replacing an item from their original order. Giving reasons for their decisions as well as asking whether it is possible to reach a single conclusion debriefs the task.

Plenary

Back to the start: This challenges pupils to reflect on the wider impact on Britain. This might be developed as separate questions for a 'poster' based answer or a mind map exercise.

Cross-curricular links

Geography: Pinpoint key locations of railway terminals in relation to the development of the railway.

ICT opportunities

History in Progress – LiveText CD 2: electronic activity

3.6 What was the impact of steam on transport?

Worksheet 3.6d Impact of the railways

Give each statement in the table below (A–H) a number to show how big a change you think the railway had on the lives of ordinary people. (1 = the biggest impact; 8 = the smallest)

Impact of the railway in 1832	Your order of impact (1–8)	Joint order of impact (1–8)
A Soldiers travel from Manchester and Liverpool in 2 hours rather than a full day's march.		
B Cheap third class tickets allowed working class people to travel by train.		
C To travel by railway was half the cost of a stage coach.		
D Goods that would go off (milk, vegetables) could be transported further than before.		
E Heavy goods (such as coal) could be carried ten times faster than canal for two-thirds the price.		
F Railways were safe after dark.		
G Goods were less likely to be stolen from a railway than from a canal.		
H The newspapers reported that there were few problems with smoke or noise from those who lived by the railway.		

Compare your list with a partner.

a) What are the similarities and differences between your lists?

b) What basis did you use to make your list? What basis did your partner use?

Agree an order with your partner and write this in the final column of the table.

3.7 What was the British Empire?

3.7a Jewel in the crown: a very British India?

Learning objectives
- To investigate and evaluate the impact of the British Empire on her colony India.
- To investigate historical issues and begin to refine their own questioning.

Historical background
The centrepiece of the British Empire was undoubtedly India. Gained in a rather haphazard way initially through the activities of the East India Company, the Indian Act of 1784 confirmed authority of the British crown over India. India provides a link between two types of imperialism. India is a consistent part of British foreign policy and was thought of as the 'jewel in the crown'. Although Queen Victoria was the Head of the Empire, she never visited. She appointed viceroys to represent her in the colonies.

Teaching Activities and Learning Outcomes

Assessment opportunity
Evaluating the effect of the British Empire on India as a colony.

Pupils will be able to
- create a report describing characteristic features of British society imposed upon India
- create a table showing arguments for and against a claim
- draw conclusions about whether the British did create a truly 'British India'.

Starter
Ask pupils to list characteristic features of Britain today. This can generate a class discussion on what features of our society make it 'British' and how these features would be accepted if imposed on another state or country. This is an excellent way to introduce the idea of a truly 'British India'.

Development
- **Green task:** Creating this report requires a straight description from contemporary sources. This activity sees the concept of a truly 'British India' from a British point of view. More able pupils will begin to question Indian reaction and possibly British arrogance.
- **Blue task:** This activity encourages pupils to see the concept of a truly 'British India' from an Indian point of view.
- **Orange task:** This task demands cross-referencing of sources to judge if Britain created a truly 'British India'. The criteria to judge success (working conditions) are new and this will encourage pupils to refine their questions about historical issues. If India assumes the negative characteristic features of Britain and shares the same defects, does this make it a truly 'British India'? This high level thinking activity requires pupils to draw their own conclusions.

Plenary
Class vote: Did Britain create a truly 'British India'. One-third of the class should explain their response from the point of view of a British viceroy; one-third should explain from an Indian point of view; and one-third third from a foreign traveller visiting both places for the first time. This should stimulate an interesting debate that encourages pupils to develop their answers in response to refined questioning.

Cross-curricular links
Geography, Citizenship.

ICT opportunities
History in Progress – LiveText CD 2: electronic activity

3.7 What was the British Empire?

3.7b The bullet that started a 'mutiny'

Learning objectives

- To investigate causes of the 'Indian Mutiny'.
- To examine how the incident has been portrayed in history.

Historical background

In 1857 there was a rebellion in northern India by Sepoy troops and Hindu and Muslim chiefs. The British called it a mutiny, but this has imperialistic tendencies. Really it should be called an Indian national uprising. After two years of fighting the uprising was eventually put down. British losses were small, but the atrocities committed by both sides affected relations between them for the next 90 years.

Teaching Activities and Learning Outcomes

Assessment opportunity

Questioning interpretations of the 'Indian Mutiny' at the time and in history books since.

Pupils should be able to

- explain, prioritise and link the multiple causes of the uprising
- highlight similarities and differences between interpretations of the uprising
- evaluate the usefulness of a piece of propaganda as a historical source and analyse the implications of the term 'mutiny' suggesting their own alternatives.

Starter

Use **Worksheet 3.7b** to assess prior knowledge on the subject of the 'Indian Mutiny'.

Development:

- **Green task:** Pupils explain, prioritise and link the multiple causes of the uprising based on prior knowledge of the aims and methods of British empire building. More able pupils will question from whose point of view should they prioritise – British or Indian? All the causes could stem from the last.
- **Blue task:** Pupils highlight similarities and differences in a modern Indian and contemporary British account of the uprising. Then they describe the differences with regard to who was committing the atrocities. The task increases in challenge as pupils try to explain the difference of opinions, and need to examine the attribution of sources and point out the nationality of the author and date of writing. More able pupils will begin to examine purpose and intended audience.
- **Orange task:** Pupils evaluate the usefulness of propaganda and explain how it reflects imperialistic tendencies and an attempt to reinforce racist feelings of superiority in the British. Pupils then move on to question the use of the word 'mutiny' to describe this uprising and suggest their own alternative title. This is a high level thinking activity that could lead to a discussion on the impact of labels of such incidents on the future relations between the countries.

Plenary

Pupils share alternative titles for the 'mutiny' that do not have imperialistic tendencies and explain their choice. Pupils reflect on the whole event in light of its new title and discuss if either side was justified.

Cross-curricular links

Citizenship.

ICT opportunities

Research impact of British colonisation on modern-day India.

History in Progress – LiveText CD 2: electronic activity

3.7 What was the British Empire?

Worksheet 3.7b The bullet that started a 'mutiny'

What do you know about the Indian Mutiny?

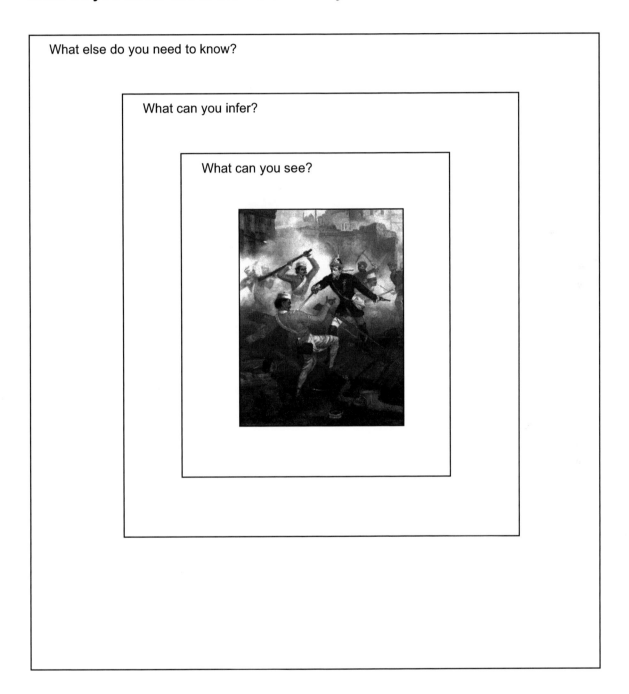

What else do you need to know?

What can you infer?

What can you see?

3.7 What was the British Empire?

3.7c The scramble for Africa

Learning objectives
- To investigate significant events in the 'scramble for Africa'.
- To identify ways in which they illustrate changing attitudes towards Empire.

Historical background
The Scramble for Africa (1870–1914) began when France and Belgium challenged British influence in Africa. Britain took full control of Egypt in 1882 ending dual control with France, but control of the Sudan became an issue, and in 1899 France recognised British supremacy. War, lasting three years, also broke out against the Boers in southern Africa. The British had fought the Dutch in South Africa earlier in 1880 and had been defeated. They agreed South Africa should be divided between the British and the Dutch, but Britain claimed overall authority. War broke out again as the Boers refused political rights for new settlers looking to exploit their gold mines. The British subjected Boer civilians to terrible conditions in concentration camps, and even though the British eventually won the whole incident was an embarrassment at home and abroad.

Teaching Activities and Learning Outcomes

Assessment opportunity

Assessing changing support for the growth of Empire by investigating significant events in Africa.

Pupils will be able to

- describe to a partner the growth of European control of Africa using maps
- analyse how the fight for the control of Egypt revealed a change in attitude for some towards Empire
- judge how the Boer War contributed to that growing change of attitude towards Empire.

Starter

Pupils use an atlas to locate Africa. Ask them to identify natural features that would make it a prize for European powers and other features that made it desirable in the context of the rest of the world.

Development

- **Green task:** This gives pupils an overview of where blocks of power were being created and will help them to understand why control of some areas, e.g. Egypt and southern Africa, was so important.
- **Blue task:** This task involves pupils investigating one of the significant events of the 'Scramble for Africa'. More able pupils will be able to judge the significance of this event both in terms of a fight for power and the awakening of the British public to the imperialistic/nationalistic tendencies.
- **Orange task:** Pupils examine a source that suggests Britain acted in a way that was contrary to the belief system it had portrayed in order to gain an empire and judge how far British actions still reflected British ideals. This task could solicit some very high order answering. It encourages pupils to judge changes in attitudes against a broader developing chronological framework and begins to blend aspects of economic and social history and their impact on declining imperialistic tendencies.

Plenary

Pupils answer three questions: What did you already know at the start of the lesson? What have you learned in this lesson? What else do you need to know? This assessment for learning opportunity can also form the basis of the starter for the next lesson. Pupils could write their responses on sticky notes and stick them on the wall to give a quick visual display of pupil feedback.

ICT opportunities

History in Progress – LiveText CD 2: electronic activity

3.7 What was the British Empire?

3.7d Taking it further!: A heroic death?

Learning objectives
- Analyse different presentations of Nelson's death and investigate why there are differences between them.

Historical background
Nelson was a celebrity and hero in his own lifetime. He had risen through the ranks of the Royal Navy to the position of Admiral. He earned respect and fame through his excellent tactics which he used on many occasions to win victories such as at the Battle of Copenhagen, the Battle of the Nile and, most famously, the Battle of Trafalgar (1805). He commanded the navy at a time of war with France and England was in desperate need of a naval hero to prevent Napoleon extending his vast empire to control England as well. Like all celebrities, Nelson found there was also much interest in his private life which some found scandalous (he left his wife for a relationship with a married beauty, Emma Hamilton).

Teaching Activities and Learning Outcomes

Assessment opportunity

Analysing the reliability of sources and accounting for different interpretations of the death of Nelson.

Pupils will be able to

- compare the impression of Nelson's death shown in two paintings
- explain why the paintings give different impressions of Nelson's death
- make a judgment about which painting gives a more realistic impression of his death.

Starter

Use **source a** (the image of Nelson's Column in London) on page 176 of *History in Progress – Book 2* to generate a list of pupils' impressions of Nelson. Give pupils some background about Nelson and his victory at the Battle of Trafalgar.

Development

- **Task 1:** Pupils begin by comparing impressions of the death of Nelson from **sources b and c** on page 176 to complete the table on **Worksheet 3.7d**. Encourage pupils to discuss the ways in which Benjamin West's portrayal of the death of Nelson seems more dramatic and heroic. Pupils might say that it occurs on open deck in the midst of battle, surrounded by many sailors makes it seem more dramatic, and that Nelson is shown in full uniform.
- **Task 2:** Pupils should consider why West made these changes and which painting is more reliable.
- **Task 3:** Pupils might find it useful to refer to **source d**, in which West explains that he felt it was important to show Nelson as having a 'heroic death' in order to encourage further admiration of him.

Plenary

Think, pair, share: Ask pupils to think about a person or event about which they think the truth has been distorted in the media. Why do they think this distortion has taken place?

ICT opportunities

History in Progress – LiveText CD 2: electronic activity

3.7 What was the British Empire?

Worksheet 3.7d A heroic death?

Compare and contrast the images of Nelson's death by Devis and West to complete the table below.

	Source b, the painting by Devis	Source c, the painting by West
Where is Nelson shown as dying?		
Roughly how many people are shown around him? What are they doing?		
What was Nelson wearing?		
How does Nelson appear? What is he doing?		

Unit 3 Moving and travelling

3.8 Making connections: Why did the ability of people to move and travel change the way they lived?

Learning objectives
- To understand that easier transportation could have positive and negative consequences for the way that people lived.
- To analyse and explain the nature and extent of diversity and change across different time periods.

Historical background
See lesson plans and enquiries throughout this unit.

Assessment opportunity

Understanding causation and analysis of the scale of effect of freer movement. Throughout this unit, pupils have been paired to complete the first two tasks. Care will be needed to tease out individual contributions to the paired activity. This might be done through observation of oral contributions in the two to four 'snowball' activities.

Pupils will be able to

- understand a sense of scale in the effect that easier travel brought in this period
- identify factors that influenced why people moved and travelled
- suggest links between specific causal factors for moving and the scale of their effect.

Starter

What would make you move from your hometown? This will produce multiple answers that you will need to be ready for. An alternative would be to ask for any barriers to people moving today. The answers can be used to reach judgements on whether the same reasons/barriers existed in the past.

Development

Green task: Pupils should be directed to the diagram on page 178 of *History in Progress – Book 2*. This exercise may need initial support in terms of open questions to help pupils recognise how widespread the effects of being able to move were.

Blue task: Pupils should be asked to review the factors to be found on the jigsaw pieces as to whether they played a significant role in why people moved in the units that they have studied. To increase the challenge the factors – including any that the pupils might have added – should be linked to the scale diagram to help pupils recognise that certain factors have greater effects than others, while still more may be influential in their effects at all levels.

Orange task: After expanding the tasks to identify possible cause and effect, this then encourages the pupils to select a single factor to explain why people moved. This should be focused in the form of a presentation and pupils should be encouraged to use evidence from all units to back up their answer.

Plenary

After the development exercises pupils could be asked to review the answers in the form of a spider diagram. Ranking the reasons on the diagram will provide further challenge.

Cross-curricular links

Geography, Citizenship.

ICT opportunities

The final activity could be completed as a short PowerPoint presentation; alternatively pupils could use a word processing/publishing package to write an extended answer.

History in Progress – LiveText CD 2: electronic activity

Unit 3 Moving and travelling

Assessment Unit 3

3.9 Assessment task 2: How had travel changed the world by 1901?

Pupils will be able to

- recognise and order enquiries in terms of the significance they had in changing the world since 1603
- evaluate sources in order to develop conclusions.

What the task is about

- The task picks up on the concept of a time machine introduced at the start of the unit. This time however, the pupil is put in the position of wondering what they should take back with them to 1603, and are therefore asked to filter their 'artefacts' for significance.
- This exercise could be done individually; however, the formative process of sharing ideas between at least two pupils will encourage them to consider the criteria they are using to make final judgements.
- Although this exercise does not have to be completed on cards, to do so would make the task more accessible. Pupils are given a straightforward task to write on each card the name of an enquiry they have completed, but are then asked to rank/scale a number of additional factors according to simple criteria. **Worksheet 3.9a** can be used to support pupils: this sheet can be photocopied as necessary, and five cards cut out and handed out to each pupil.
- The discussion that this process produces should be utilised to challenge pupils about their understanding of a particular aspect and how it relates to individual enquiries.
- The completed cards can be used in a number of ways. Individuals can place them along the table in a rank order of significance to identify the five 'artefacts' they would take back to the past. However, an alternative to this would be to collect up and redistribute cards relating to a given enquiry in order to challenge pupils to reflect on whether what has been written on the 'new' card is accurate in their understanding, before placing it on the significance line.
- The assessment should close with pupils producing an individual piece of work identifying their five top 'artefacts'. Sharing the markscheme with pupils before they complete the written piece allows both teacher and pupil to identify clearly what has been achieved and what more needs to be completed to reach a given level.
- Images from this unit can be accessed via the Livetext resource bank.
- A markscheme is provided on **Worksheet 3.9b**.

Unit 3 Assessment 3

Worksheet 3.9a

How had travel changed the world by 1901?: Assessment cards

Lesson title

Circle where these changes happened

locally / nationally / internationally

What was the key point? What happened to people in this lesson?

Circle how different life was for people as a result of the changes that happened

very different / different / not very different

How important were these changes?

(scale between 1–10, with 1 being very important)

1	2	3	4	5	6	7	8	9	10

Lesson title

Circle where these changes happened

locally / nationally / internationally

What was the key point? What happened to people in this lesson?

Circle how different life was for people as a result of the changes that happened

very different / different / not very different

How important were these changes?

(scale between 1–10, with 1 being very important)

1	2	3	4	5	6	7	8	9	10

Lesson title

Circle where these changes happened

locally / nationally / internationally

What was the key point? What happened to people in this lesson?

Circle how different was life for people as a result of the changes that happened

very different / different / not very different

How important were these changes?

(scale between 1–10, with 1 being very important)

1	2	3	4	5	6	7	8	9	10

Lesson title

Circle where these changes happened

locally / nationally / internationally

What was the key point? What happened to people in this lesson?

Circle how different was life for people as a result of the changes that happened

very different / different / not very different

How important were these changes?

(scale between 1–10, with 1 being very important)

1	2	3	4	5	6	7	8	9	10

Unit 3 Assessment 2

Worksheet 3.9b
How had travel changed the world by 1901?

How did you do?

Level 4 I was able to …	
describe some features of the period.	
say that they are important.	
identify a reason why change happened and a consequence of that change.	

Level 5 I was able to …	
describe some of the main features of the period.	
begin to be aware of why some events, people and changes might be judged as more significant than others.	
use selected information to explain why events or people were important.	
select and use appropriate historical words to support and structure your work.	

Level 6 I was able to …	
begin to show that I understand why conclusions about the importance of events, people and changes have been made.	
explain the way those conclusions have been reached.	
select, organise and use relevant information, using the right historical words to produce structured work.	

Things I did well: _____

I need to learn more about: _____

One thing I need to improve is: _____

I will do this by: _____

Teacher comment: _____

_____

Pupil comment: _____

_____